D1562137

Adrian Waller

1975

LITTLEFIELD, ADAMS & CO.   Totowa, New Jersey

Theatre on a shoestring

First published in the United States 1975 by

LITTLEFIELD, ADAMS & CO.

by special arrangement with Clarke, Irwin & Co., Ltd.

© 1972 by Clarke, Irwin & Company Limited

Printed in Canada

Library of Congress Cataloging in Publication Data

Waller, Adrian
   Theatre on a Shoestring

   (A Littlefield, Adams Quality Paperback No. 295)
   Bibliography: p.
   1. Amateur theatricals.   I. Title.
PN3151.W3 1975   792'.0222   75-2262
ISBN 0-8226-0295-4

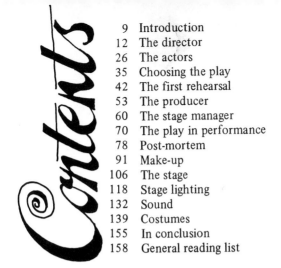

Contents

Acknowledgements

The author would like to thank the following persons and organizations who helped in the development of this book:

The Canadian Opera Company; Malabar Ltd.; Max Factor Ltd., of Toronto and Hollywood, California; make-up artist Mrs. Hilda Healy; Miss Murielle-Dolores McCabe, of Burlington, Ontario; Rank Strand Electric Ltd., of London, England, and Strand Century Ltd., of Toronto; Randolph Rhodes; *The Spectator,* Hamilton, Ontario (particularly Stewart Brown); The Stratford Festival, Ontario; TABS, a world-wide magazine for theatre technicians; and Miss Jacqueline Willetts who typed the manuscript.

Adrian Waller has written a very useful and readable book which should be of interest and value to amateur theatre groups, to students and to drama enthusiasts generally.

The author pinpoints many of the problems that inevitably arise when plays are produced on a limited budget, and points out how these difficulties may be surmounted. He stresses the fact that it is not necessary to have tremendous sums behind a production for it to be artistically effective. Ingenuity and taste will often supply the necessary ingredients.

Mr. Waller also emphasizes the importance of technique and the necessity for mastering the small details which contribute so much to the success of a performance. And he makes the point that technique is not the province of the actors alone, but of the director, stage manager, stage hands, wardrobe mistress—indeed everyone involved in the production.

This book is not, however, a dull recital of facts. It has a brightness which makes it entertaining reading. Nor is it only the amateur or professional participant who will derive enjoyment and instruction from this book. The theatre-loving layman who has little knowledge of what goes on behind the scenes from the moment a play is chosen to the moment it is performed will also find *Theatre on a Shoestring* fascinating and informative reading.

GRATIEN GÉLINAS

Montreal
August, 1972

Dedicated to a man named Douglas Maugham who fixes lights, hammers nails in sets, makes doors and fireplaces, does the sound, sells tickets to all his friends . . . and acts.

Drama is the oldest and the greatest of all the arts. It begins before man has even learned to speak and provides the simplest means of communication between mortals, conveying the profoundest or the subtlest of meanings to the most educated or the most uneducated of men. Until we have solved all the mysteries of the universe it will remain the only form of communication that can adequately deal with great riddles. Drama celebrates the magnificent struggle of mankind to achieve enlightenment, but if theatre-going were confined to the local Little Theatre group's annual repertoire of pot-boilers, it might never be guessed.

Of course there's no harm in presenting the so-called pot-boilers. They've become termed as such because audiences have liked them and whatever is being offered must be done with one initial aim—to please the public. But generally, and in a book of this kind it's only possible to talk in very general terms, whatever is being offered by an amateur group either fails or is only a partial success. The basic reasons are usually:

Lack of talent on stage and/or behind the scenes
Lack of knowledge on stage and/or behind the scenes
Combination of both

A discerning theatre-goer wanting to be more specific could break these down even further. Lack of talent speaks for itself and is the most common factor in amateur dramatic failure, but lack of knowledge may begin with choosing a play not technically feasible and analysing or assessing it incorrectly. Add to this such frequent misdemeanours as bad casting, make-up and costumes, poor positioning of stage lighting, unimaginative directing and a set that complements neither the mood nor the atmosphere, and it shouldn't be difficult to see that the odds are much against amateurs. They are, however, often victims of their own circumstances. Most Little Theatre groups I know fail to utilize sensibly the talent that is available to them (although talent, as I stress repeatedly throughout this book, can't by any stretch of the imagination be learned, let alone from any kind of publication). They often tend to think that so long as they achieve what is good for themselves it will automatically be acclaimed by other people. More important, they often fail to master the great scheme of cohesion so necessary if a play is to be presented with all strings firmly tied . . . and artistically.

It's worth talking more about this. Some time ago while lecturing a group of college drama students, I likened the personnel involved in the presentation of a theatrical production to the components of a television set. The director, his actors, the stage manager, the producer and his technical staff each represented a tube. The picture and sound were what the audience heard and saw. Since the infallible television set had yet to be invented, I said, there would always be some distortion. Distortion, however, came in degrees and its severity depended on what component had become ineffective, weak or lazy. So it is with theatre. Drama is widening its frontiers and in so doing sometimes makes excessive demands not only upon the actors, but upon those who toil backstage as well. If, as tubes, they weaken, the people involved in a theatrical production will present their audience with a distorted picture. This distortion may be sufficient to mark it either a complete and utter failure on the one hand, or only a partial success on the other.

Like professional theatre, Little Theatre cannot afford failure. Financially speaking, it can mean bankruptcy to the professional company. To the amateur company, however, it's invariably nothing that a good rummage sale or a wine and cheese party can't put right. But failure in the theatre has repercussions other than financial; however brilliant the last production of the season promises to be, an audience disappointed twice may never return for more.

Furthermore, there's another facet to consider. Schools have a two-fold purpose in producing drama—to encourage an academic appreciation of the literature, and to give the student an opportunity for self-expression before an audience. It's debatable as to which is the more valuable and I do not intend to enter an opinion within the confines of this small book, except to say that provided both are accomplished the play will generally have been worthwhile. Little Theatre claims both these objectives, plus one more: it sets out to make money by asking its audience to pay. This alone necessitates and stipulates a highly conscientious approach to amateur theatre—in every department.

Usually, the excuses for defeat amongst amateurs are, "The play was too highbrow for our audiences and they didn't understand it" or, "We've got funny audiences in our area and they don't like anything that was written before 1926." What nonsense! It's true that audiences at times reveal apathetic discernment, but they're not completely shallow. If anything, they're far more perceptive than audiences of yesteryear, and are becoming increasingly aware that the theatre's power as a communicative form can surpass that of the preacher. They may not know why they liked a particular play or why they disliked it and, for the survival of some groups, amateur or professional, this is sometimes just as well. It's a fairly safe assumption though, and one on which I work myself, that, if you give an audience good theatrical literature and present it well, it will be highly satisfied. Sometimes, provided it is presented well, an audience will be highly satisfied with poor theatrical literature!

Choosing the play therefore becomes one of the most vital aspects of successful drama, especially as far as the Little Theatre group is concerned. I believe there is an art in this which should not be undermined. So much has to be considered and for this reason I have made the choosing of a play the basis for one entire chapter.

There's something else which regulates the quality and ultimate success of theatre—money, and this is saved or made, whichever way you want to look at it, by ingenuity. Unfortunately, the majority of Little Theatre groups are not noted for their ingenuity, hence they cut their profits by buying instead of making. Quite often it's a case of not knowing where a simple invention may be utilized. Where possible, I try to reveal the financial shortcuts, as well as those that save time. These are, in many ways, just as important.

Theatre on a shoestring has, by necessity, to be simple. But it need never be untidy. I know young women who are compelled to dress on a shoestring every day of their lives and somehow they always manage to look dynamic. They buy what suits them and place the emphasis upon simplicity. Their jewellery is sparse and well-chosen and, I'm told, they make enterprising studies of local stores to find out what good articles of clothing are being sold at the lowest possible prices. If they can't buy what they want, they make it, and their wardrobes are such that they contain many combinations or variations. In brief, they have mastered the art of providing a favourable illusion on the little money they can afford.

Theatre can be like that, too—especially theatre on a shoestring.

1) The Director

What he should be, what he should know, how he should prepare.

Ask an ordinary member of an audience what the director actually does and he won't have the faintest idea. To him, the director is merely a name on the front of the programme. Yet for all this, when the director is absent the audience is the first to miss him. For it is he who is largely responsible for the success or failure of the play. He interprets the author's meaning and, by skilfully blending the acting, lighting and setting into one harmonious entity, brings the play to life.

The director is primarily responsible for man oeuvring his actors about the stage like chess pieces, synchronizing where and how they go with what they have to say. To do this, he must be well acquainted with the theatre's many facets. Compare him, if you like, with the conductor of a symphony orchestra, but remember that the conductor is seen at every performance because he's on stage to share the accolades. The stage director, on the other hand, has done his work by the time the audience arrives. Opening night should find him watching the work he's put in over the past few weeks from the back of the theatre auditorium. The last time a director has anything to do with a production, other than to offer the odd piece of advice during performances, is at the dress rehearsal. From then on the stage manager takes command.

It is the stage manager's responsibility to see that the actors are standing in the stage wings in plenty of time for their entrances, and that the sound and lighting effects run smoothly and accurately against the action. But we will talk more about this important figure later.

What, I'm often asked, are the necessary qualities for a good director? Three are absolutely essential:

Imagination and sensitivity
An instinct for the dramatic or a natural sense of theatre
An eye for the pictorial

These qualities must be inborn. They cannot be learned. You can read every book that has ever been published on the technique of directing and you will acquire a great deal of knowledge. But unless you have a natural ability for the art you will be unable to put it all into focus. You will accumulate instead a long list of do's and don't's. You will learn, for example, how to group people, preventing them from standing in straight lines (and, believe me, there's nothing harder on the audience's eye than a straight line), and many hundreds

Overleaf:
Full use is made of the stage in this spectacular scene from the University of Alberta's *Marat Sade*.

13

of other traps that must be avoided. You will also probably learn that the human speaking voice, like the singing voice, has top notes and low notes, and that tension can be put into dramatic moments of a play by creating pauses of the right length at the right moments. There is no book available, however, that can help you create a specific picture, tension or rhythm in the dialogue for the specific play you might be directing at the time. Only you know what you want for your play and no amount of reading can help you produce the ingredients you and your actors are expected to "feel." They come from within—a product of the soul—and in a later chapter I will try to explain how a cast and a director can work together to bring these out.

Visually, the director sees the proscenium arch as a huge frame into which he must put a series of pictures that move gently or violently, depending on what the actors say. These pictures must always be significant to a mood which the play sets out to convey. In this respect, crowd scenes are always difficult because the director is primarily concerned with balancing his stage and creating his pictures and, at the same time, keeping the focus of attention upon important characters. He has to ensure that every actor in his crowd is part of what is going on. Each must either react to what is being said or look as though their oblivion is part of the scene. None must at any time appear to have been sent on stage by their wives to keep them out of the way.

Alas, amateur crowd scenes often have people who slip comfortably into this category. Usually they have been engaged solely to swell the ranks, and look that way because the director has not taken time to explain why they are there and how they fit into the story. Sometimes, if directors explained more to relatively insignificant performers, their productions would gain dimension and provide a more realistic and exciting environment for the principal actors.

By way of example, let's look at the first act of George Bernard Shaw's *Pygmalion*. When the curtain rises, Mrs. Eynsford Hill begins a conversation with her daughter, Clara. Soon, her son Freddy appears. The dialogue continues. Later, Eliza the flower girl, Professor Higgins and Colonel Pickering join the trio and, together, these six actors lay the foundation of the play and do a great deal to further the plot. But what is going on in the background is of equal importance. Here, Shaw introduces a group of bystanders to provide both colour and atmosphere. They are not only there to help the visual aspects of the scene, but also to make a harsh comparison between people who draw a meagre living from selling in Covent Garden Market, where the scene is set, and those more affluent, who can afford to go to the ballet. If this comparison is to be apparent to the audience, each bystander must be a carefully-etched character in the way he dresses, stands, moves and speaks. With concentration, the bystander can assume his own attitude to the situation—an attitude that will give the scene its mood. It doesn't just depend on how still he stands or on how well he remembers his moves, because acting, as I explain later, is more than this. It depends on how he smokes his pipe or cigarette, how he holds his newspaper or adjusts his cap—the kind of mannerisms best learned by watching similar real-life characters on street corners, trains and buses, in the busy world in which we lead our daily lives.

This, in part, is how a director learns his craft—by being an observer of people. He must watch their emotions and learn how they react in varying circumstances. The moment he ceases to see how people live around him, he loses contact with his world and is ultimately handicapped when he tries to carve real characters on stage.

I cannot stress this firmly enough. All my life I have been trying to see the rest of the world. It was on a train as a child, for instance, that I first noticed the different ways in which men smoke pipes. Make the study yourself sometime and you will see that old men hold them precariously in their front teeth, because by the time they've reached eighty they have no teeth at the sides and back. Younger men usually grip their pipes confidently in side teeth, and are able to leave them there while they speak. I've also spent many hours watching people waiting for buses, bracing themselves against spiteful winter winds. I've sat in doctors' offices trying to predict, by their expressions, from what each man, woman and child was suffering. Once, while directing Lucille Fletcher's potent little one-act American drama, *Sorry, Wrong Number,* I took time off from a rehearsal and sat for two hours in a telephone exchange so I could see how the operators dealt with each caller, for this is what the play was all about. They were mechanical, unemotional and, for the most part, annoyingly nonchalant—a characteristic I was able to inject into my own production, giving it more depth and credibility, as I will illustrate later.

Other qualities imperative for a director may be cultivated. These are a sympathetic understanding of human nature, tact, patience, powers of leadership, a sense of rhythm, a sense of humour and technical knowledge. Add them to those which have to be inborn and you will understand why the director is a rare being. But do not despair. A potential director may be in your group at this very moment, anxiously awaiting the opportunity to show what he can do. Let him do it, but make sure you have the right person, and not one who is offering his services out of the kindness of his heart because there is no one else, or because he thinks that directing is merely a matter of getting people on and off the stage.

Let's assume, however, that you have a director and you are prepared to let him mount a production. First, he must read the play and ask himself whether its theme is moving or exciting, without having just intellectual appeal. He must then examine the plot and decide whether it is dramatic and worthy of the theme. If the answer to one or both of these questions is "No," he would be wise to discard the play.

But let's suppose the answer is "Yes." At his first reading the director has unconsciously assumed the role of the audience. He is letting the theme of the play make an impact on his mind—just as he hopes it will later make an impact on his audience.

He should discover early that the tempo of a play does not remain constant. Just as the needle of a seismograph oscillates violently during an earthquake, so the rhythm of a play moves up and down in moments of conflict or emotion. The peaks are called climaxes. During his next reading, the director's dramatic instinct should be at work noting where these climaxes occur. To clarify the shape of the play in his mind, he may decide to make a graph. Taking the normal tempo as his central line, he should note on his graph any deviation above or below this. He will see, then, that although the play has one big climax, there are also a series of lesser climaxes; that a scene has a climax, as does a passage between two people, and even an individual speech. Within the ascending curve of the play towards its final great moment, there may be a series of upward and downward movements on the graph. The downward movement, however, should never quite return to the level of the beginning of the play.

Note the sensible positioning. The actress needs all the visual emphasis she can get for her scene in *Light Up the Sky* (staged by the Metro Theatre Centre, Vancouver).

Let me take the beginning of the murder scene from *Macbeth,* by way of illustration. Macbeth, within the castle, is about to murder Duncan. Lady Macbeth enters, and by her mood and words she creates suspense in the minds of the audience, so that the scene is played in steadily mounting tension. Suddenly there is a cry within and, with this, a violent upward leap in tension. Although that level is not maintained throughout subsequent speeches, the drop is slight, and never goes back to the level of the beginning of the scene. On "Why did you bring these daggers?" there is another sharp upward curve which is maintained until the exit of the Macbeths. With the entrance of the porter the tension declines, but to prevent an anticlimax by too sudden a fall, the persistent knocking continues.

As he reads, it should become obvious to the director that these moments of climax centre upon certain characters in the play, and that the greatest climax involves the principal figure. Now is the time to study the characters and their relation to the theme and plot. The director will see that the principal character is very strongly associated with the theme and that the main plot revolves around him. Additionally, he will find that there are a number of subsidiary plots, each of which develops some aspect of the theme. There are also a number of other characters, each of whom throws light upon the principals. In nearly all well-written plays there is usually only one principal character, and the main plot stands out clearly. The director must make sure that the audience's attention is directed towards the main plot and that the lesser characters are not given undue prominence, otherwise the balance of the play will be destroyed. This is particularly important when a strong actor is playing a minor role.

The director should now be considering how he is going to present the play to the audience, so that it is aware of the underlying themes and the significant moments throughout. He has to create and maintain a dramatic illusion in order that the audience will believe and accept what it sees and hears on stage. When planning the settings he should bear in mind that their purpose is to assist the actor in creating an illusion, and not to hinder him. His grouping and movement, which must never be haphazard, should also have particular significance at moments of climax.

This again is where the director's dramatic and pictorial instincts come into play. Conflict and contrast are the essence of drama, and he must use these to their greatest effect in moments of climax. His dramatic sense will tell him how pregnant a moment of stillness can be in the midst of noise, or a shrill scream piercing a silence, or a quick outburst following a slow, heavy remark. His pictorial eye will recognize the effectiveness of one figure isolated from a group—a standing figure among a group of prostrate ones, a motionless figure in a scene of movement. He will realize, too, that this contrast can be carried into costume and lighting; someone wearing black will stand out from a group in colour, and one bright splash of colour in a sombre scene will catch the eye.

Long before the play is cast, the director should have consulted his set designer, and together they should have made plans for the scenery by making a scale model of the set. When no set designer is available, the director must do this job himself. If the scale model, whoever produces it, is accurate and shows furniture, the director can then detect any problems he might have later through lack of acting space. He will be able to group his actors and visualize their moves more easily, thus avoiding such stage sins as "masking" and "scissors." The masking of actors occurs when one stands before the other, and blocks the audience's view, thus spoiling the visual effect. "Scissors" results when two actors cross the stage simultaneously, leaving the audience, through optical illusion, staring at the point at which their paths crossed.

Even before the first rehearsal, the director should have written all his moves in his script so he can direct his actors unhesitatingly and inspire them with confidence. He should not, however, be too rigid about this. He may find that while some of his planned "blocking" is effective on paper, it is less effective on stage and must be changed. Besides, the director who boasts that he has everything solidly planned in his mind before he begins rehearsals does not allow for later imaginative developments, either in himself or his actors.

I like to think of a production blossoming like a flower. Even though it may look impressive in its earlier stages, it must always have room to develop further. It must gain colour and vitality through the enthusiasm of those taking part. A director who is too rigid about what he thinks, and who fails to listen to what others have to say, kills incentive and dulls the spirit. This is where his qualities of tact and leadership come into force. A

21

director must play his actors with a slack line, particularly at the beginning, bringing them gently to shore. But he must not be afraid to give the line an occasional jerk to let them know that he is on the other end. He should try to draw something out of his actors rather than thrust something in. The dictator never gets the best from his actors, but neither does the director who is afraid of them.

The experienced director may prefer to ignore the "acting edition" of plays, and work out for himself the setting and the movement. But these editions can be very helpful to the less experienced director, providing he uses them sensibly. The acting edition is often printed from the prompt copy of the original production. The directions are sound, but the amateur director must not follow them blindly. He must not accept a move unless he fully understands the reason for it. He should also remember that the moves and settings were originally planned for a stage in either London or New York—a stage probably six times the size of his own—so that to reproduce all the moves may make his play too restless, and to adopt similar settings may be impossible in such a confined space.

Only once can I recall keeping rigidly to the moves in my acting edition. That was when I directed *Pygmalion* in Toronto in 1964. George Bernard Shaw, I decided, had an unerring sense of when and why an actor should move, and no matter how much I wanted to try things my way, I always came back to what Shaw had originally written in his manuscript.

Several times, however, I've adjusted an author's conception of a set to fit my own stage. An example of this occurred when I directed Neil Simon's brilliant comedy, *The Odd Couple,* in 1966. The script called for five entrances: a front entrance into an apartment, as well as doors leading off into a kitchen, two bedrooms and a washroom. My set designer and I read the play several times and saw no reason why two of the entrances—those to the bedrooms—could not be eliminated by designing the interior in such a way that the audience saw two corridors, one leading to the kitchen and the other leading to the bedrooms. The corridors meant we could avoid having more doors than I wanted on the set. I have never liked doors. Too many actors have the annoying habit of trying to open them the wrong way in front of an audience.

I also made an adjustment to the set in my

23

Toronto production of the Keith Waterhouse-Willis Hall play, *Billy Liar,* in 1964. The script called for a two-room set—a modest living room and the hall outside. It also called for a staircase that led down to a front door which had to be visible to the audience. Needless to say, the expense of the set was well outside the scope of the group for which I was directing. The London company which originally presented the play could afford the luxury of Billy making his first entrance, a strong one, down the staircase. We couldn't, so I played the action effectively in one room, with one entrance. The audience accepted that this entrance led to a hall outside, from which the characters could move either into the kitchen or, by turning the other way, to the stairs. I also decided that the front door could open into the living room because there are still houses being built this way in England today. At any rate, the set was workable and the production did not suffer too severely from these amendments.

These set modifications should serve to show that a good director is one who has courage to make changes to a script and, if necessary, to cut it. I have never directed a play without finding some good reason to chop out long passages of dialogue. As skilful as they may be in developing plots and presenting dialogue, playwrights are not directors. Their plays have faults, though not always serious, which have to be spotted and rectified. Long before I began directing *Pygmalion,* for instance, I decided that the fifth and last act was far too long. Shaw had Henry Higgins frequently repeating himself in a chain of rather cumbersome speeches which I ruthlessly began cutting down, tightening the last act and helping the play to enjoy more of an upward curve to the final climax.

I am frequently asked by potential directors, especially those who have never themselves set foot on stage as performers, whether it is imperative for a director to have been an actor. My reply is an unhesitating "No." Several highly competent directors I consult from time to time (and a director should always have the humility to seek the advice of another) would die of fright, even if they only had to stand in the centre stage doorway and deliver the cliché line, "Dinner is served." But they are artists at provoking others to do what they can't themselves. It is probably true, however, that a director has less difficulty in relating to his actors if he were once one himself. He would be more suitably equipped to assess capabilities and "feel" those dramatic pauses. As a performer, he might even have experienced that supremely joyous moment which comes from the correct timing of a laugh line. And that, I must add, is something else you cannot really learn. It just has to be "felt."

Reading List

Cole and Chinoy, eds., *Directors on Directing* (Bobbs-Merrill).
Fernald, John, *The Play Produced* (Deane).
Hunt, Hugh, *The Director in the Theatre* (Routledge and Kegan Paul).
Hunt, Hugh, *Old Vic Prefaces* (Routledge and Kegan Paul).

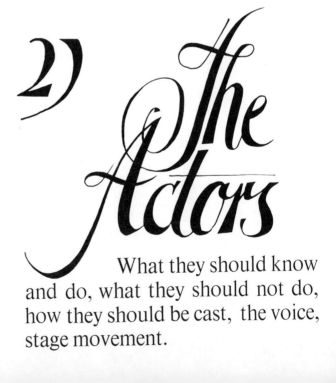

2) The Actors

What they should know and do, what they should not do, how they should be cast, the voice, stage movement.

Most people join Little Theatre because they want to act. Acting has an irresistible appeal for the young, the old, the timid and the exhibitionist alike. It is always exciting when you are in a play that exposes talent housed in the most unlikely exterior. I've seen well-rounded, intelligent performances by people who, in real life, are almost completely inarticulate. I've also seen the work of grandmothers and young children who have never before set foot on stage. Alas, I fear, it is also true that some of the most determined, enthusiastic actors on the amateur stage are those who have no talent at all.

The essential qualities of an actor are, I believe:

Imagination
Sensitivity
Dramatic instinct

As in the case of the director, these qualities may be latent, but they must be there in the first place. Technique can and must be learned, but it is of limited use without the three basic qualities. They help the actor create on stage a character that is far removed from himself in real life. They help him move, speak and think as someone else and this is what acting really is. In the final analysis, the most competent actor is the one able to combine his technique with the three basic qualities.

When an actor is cast for the part of, say, Jack Willetts, he should first of all read the whole play. What the other people in the play say about the character and the way he behaves in certain situations will tell the actor a great deal about the man he is to portray. The actor must seek the motive for the man's actions, and realize that although the play may be concerned with a few hours or days of a man's life, he has had a previous existence which may account for some of the traits in his character. Now the play may tell us nothing at all of Jack Willetts' past life, so this is where the actor's imagination comes into play. He must build for himself a complete background. He must ask himself what the man is like inside and out. Next he must begin to give life to the character, and here he has two courses open to him. He can take the character, which as yet has no life, and step inside, using his own body to make Jack Willetts a real person. Or he may have a very clear picture in his mind of exactly what the character should look like—probably taken from a real-life study—and by close observation of the nature and habits of his model, begin to build, working from the outside to the inside. This latter way, however, is somewhat dangerous because it can lead to superficial acting.

Once in the "skin" of the character, the actor must begin to move and speak as Jack Willetts. He should imagine what Mr. Willetts is feeling, and how this will affect his appearance. As far as he can, he should draw on the memory of his own emotions, and apply them to those of his character. For instance, supposing Jack Willetts is entering his prize canary into a bird show and, when he comes to take his bird away, finds instead that it has been eaten by a cat. His feelings will be a mixture of frustration at being unable to enter the bird for competition, grief for the little bird, and anger against the cat. The actor may never have kept a canary in his life, but there must have been many occasions when he experienced this mixture of emotions. He should recall one of these occasions and try to recall how he himself behaved and what his physical sensations were, so that when he plays the cat-and-the-canary scene his thoughts will fly back to the real incident, and he will automatically react, physically, in the same way. Of course there may be many situations for which the actor cannot find a parallel in his own life. The classic illustration always given is that of a murderer. The actor has probably never experienced the feelings of a murderer. But is that quite true? Don't we all feel murderous towards the wasp when it is persistently buzzing round us? Isn't the murder of a human being the same sensation magnified a thousand times? When the actor has no parallel on which to draw, then he must rely upon his imagination.

All this, of course, requires concentration and observation, coupled with vivid imagination. Now the actor's technique must be brought to bear on the character. His body and speech must be sufficiently fluent to express externally the emotions he is feeling internally. He must move and speak as the character, and he must be able to project this character to the back of the theatre. This is where so many amateur actors come to grief, for although they may be feeling the emotions quite sincerely, their untrained bodies are unable to express them truly. The result is what appear to be insincere performances.

On other occasions, the movements, speech and emotions of the role are so small that the performances are colourless. This is where the actor must use his dramatic instinct. He must be able to sense what is "good theatre," and to have a feeling of unity with the audience. It is not enough to be absolutely natural on the stage—it must be an illusion of naturalness, and not the real thing. A certain amount of physical effort is required, and amateurs are apt to forget this. Every move must have a beginning, a middle and, most important of all, an end. So often a move begins well and then trails away in indecision. An actor who has been rehearsing in a small room may forget that he must be overheard by a third person—the audience.

It is a good thing for him to imagine his speech as a kind of boomerang which, when it leaves his mouth, circles the audience to the back of the pit before reaching the man opposite him on the stage. He must learn to breathe well and deeply, for poor tone and lack of projection are caused primarily by faulty breathing. He must be sure, too, that his articulation is clear. There are many helpful books on speech, but, in the first instance, he should consult a speech expert because speech faults are difficult to detect in oneself.

An actor needs great variety in the pitch of his voice. A trained actor often has a vocal range of two octaves, but the average person rarely uses more than an octave in ordinary speaking. It is not easy for the untrained voice to achieve this variety. But there is one variety of voice which can be mastered and that is variety of pace. This is extremely important, but is often ignored in amateur performances.

If you stop and think about it, the actor's greatest weapon in selling his art to his audience is his voice. If he has a bad one, his audience will soon lose interest in what he has to say. You will, I'm sure, agree that there is nothing worse than having to sit through three acts of deadpan mumbling from a principal character. That's why, when I cast my own plays, I pay special attention to people with interesting voices. Quite often I can overlook a speech impediment, depending upon its severity, because some impediments lend charm and can often be incorporated into certain characterizations. More than anything else I want resonance in a voice, because it is this that decides whether or not it will be heard at the back of the theatre. When I tell an actor to project, I do not merely mean, "Speak up!"—as is the usual interpretation of the word. I am asking him to focus his voice. I want him to support it with breath so that it becomes brighter in its tone, and more penetrating.

Note this lively tea party scene from *Sailor Beware!* The onus is upon the actress (standing) to avoid being masked by the others, sitting. This scene also shows the effective use of an actor's back.

The actor must also learn repose on stage. This is born of a relaxed body and a mind fully concentrated on the play. Novices often worry because they are required to stand still for minutes on end. They fidget. They don't know what to do with their hands. They drift upstage into a position they think has taken them out of the eye of the audience but has, in fact, taken them to a point of greater visual strategy. The director must help them to concentrate, and must try to impress upon them the importance of listening and reacting to what other characters are saying. The audience's attention should always be directed to the focal point of the scene, and if a small-part actor allows his attention to wander, and fidgets, he will draw to himself the attention of the audience, something he is striving so earnestly to avoid.

Once the play is in rehearsal, the director should try to avoid giving advice or instruction in voice production or movement. This only makes the actor even more self-conscious than he might have been when first he accepted the part. A private and tactful word in the actor's ear about sounding his consonants or unclenching his jaw is more salutary than a public reprimand, which can be embarrassing. Of course, if it is a case of misinterpretation either in speech or movement, the correction must be done publicly and quickly—before it becomes a habit.

One of the director's most complex tasks is that of casting. If he makes a mistake here he may never be able to redeem it. That's why large movie companies, which have far more money to lose than amateur theatre groups, engage perceptive experts to help the director select his cast. When it is left, however, to one man in an amateur drama group (as it should be, for executives and committees must never interfere) casting is a job to be done carefully, honestly and with the fullest possible knowledge of the play and the type of vehicle it is.

Generally, a director must first look for "type." I do not submit to the argument that ability should be his first consideration. It matters not how technically-competent an actor might be. In the amateur theatre, as I have already pointed out, the actor is usually limited in the number of personal characteristics he can discard in the creation of his stage character. If the part in question calls for a large man with a bald head and a voice of thunder, it would be a mistake to use a performer without these obviously essential physical marks. I would much rather find the right man for the role by casting outside the group—even to the point of finding someone inexperienced but keen, and equipping him, through rehearsals, with sufficient technique to master the role. Of course, if the role makes excessive dramatic demands on the novice and the physical aspects are secondary, I would then face the possibility of using my best, large actor, helping him vocally, and asking the make-up department to try to hide his hair. With luck, I might even get him to shave his head, although such dedication is relatively unheard of in the amateur theatre!

Looking initially for type is a methodical, sensible way of casting. It limits the temptation to use people you know to be competent, keen and reliable, however unsuitable they might be for the parts you are trying to fill.

If he has been a keen observer of people, the director will be exercising his eye for the visual, even at this early stage, by looking at actors available to him at auditions, and gathering ideas about using some of them purely for any physical defects or attributes they might have. This is very important. A play can cease to convince if everyone in it is unusually or unnecessarily handsome. This applies particularly to crowd scenes. While casting *Pygmalion*, I spent several weeks looking for fat women and men with interesting beards and moustaches to set among my bystanders in the opening scene. One of the figures was a man with a bulbous nose and withered hand. He was not called upon to speak. All he had to do was stand and watch the action. He added a glow of reality to the scene—simply by being there.

Conversely, if a script calls for glamour, then the director must find it, or at least do the best he can. In the amateur theatre, however, the best a director can do for his audience is not always good enough. I have seen the most voluminous women on stage—even in such roles as Elvira, in Noel Coward's *Blithe Spirit*. Coward says that Elvira must float, not walk. She has returned from the dead and is seen now in spirit form. She must also contrast with Ruth, the other leading woman, by being very pleasant to look at. Unfortunately, the woman I once saw play Elvira had a face that would stop a clock. Carried away by the comedy, she cavorted on stage and persisted in strutting through the entire three acts. The audience thought she was hilarious. She was, indeed, though not quite as Coward had intended!

Just as unsuitable was the woman of no meagre acreage I saw as the girl who gets her man in that warm, sensitive American comedy, *The Tender Trap*. Most of her bulk stretched uncompromisingly from side to side which meant that she filled the doorway on her first entrance. The credibility fell out of her relationship with the leading man because she stood like an oak tree defying the woodman's saw—three inches above him. Again, the audience thought it was hilarious, even at moments when the play made serious statements about loneliness and promiscuity. But what was being laughed at? The person playing the role was the source of comedy, rather than the character he or she was trying to portray. This is known as "grass roots" theatre, and is born of people playing roles for which they are physically unsuited, usually to the extreme. One man is to blame—the director.

Casting in small groups can be disconcertingly political, and a director is therefore called upon to exercise his qualities of tact and regard for human nature. He may have to decide that because Mrs. Brown played the leading part in the last play, Mrs. Black should be given the principal part in the next, while Mrs. Brown helps backstage. This I am sure is the right idea, for it encourages team spirit and shows the actor that he represents only one facet of dramatic art. There must be one proviso, however—that Mrs. Black is suitable for the part. In fairness to the audience, suitability for the part must be the essential test. One difficult problem may be whether to give an important part to an experienced actress even though she is too old, or whether the part should go to a young but inexperienced girl. The director must, of course, decide for himself, but I would advise him not to underestimate the attraction of youth. If the younger woman has freshness and personality I should feel inclined to risk it, even though she may be technically inexperienced. If, however, she lacks personality to sustain the part and is in danger of giving a colourless performance, I should then cast the experienced actress—providing her voice and figure are young enough. Nothing is more embarrassing than to see a middle-aged woman playing a part for which she is obviously too old.

Directors should also remember that because someone reads well, it does not necessarily follow that he is a good actor. It often happens in reverse—good actors may be poor readers. A simple test in assessing dramatic ability is to ask actors to read the high points in a script. Question how deeply they can emote, and watch for:

A sense of style
Concentration
An ability to articulate and use the voice range
An understanding of the dialogue

When I cast a play I go quite deeply into the characterizations so that everyone who auditions knows exactly what is expected of him. He cannot then say, "I didn't get the part because I didn't know what the director wanted." I even want to see how well my actors move, especially when I'm considering them for major roles. When casting a man for the zany part of Victor Velasco in *Barefoot in the Park*, I asked him to go down on all fours and bark like a dog so I could measure his inhibitions. On other occasions I have been known to ask actors to sing, even though the script has not required it of them. During my auditions for *The Sound of Music*, little children so keen to get a part and having already sung something from the show, volunteered to perform farmyard noises and go through tap dance routines. Don't let this surprise you. Children are far less inhibited than adults.

Reading List

Cole, Toby and Chinoy, Helen, eds., *Actors on Acting* (Crown).

Darlington, W. A., *The Actor and His Audience* (Phoenix House).

Goodman, Edward, *Make Believe: The Art of Acting* (Scribner).

Lewis, Robert, *Method or Madness* (Samuel French). `

Redgrave, Michael, *An Actor's Ways and Means* (Heinemann).

Redgrave, Michael, *Mask or Face* (Heinemann).

Ross, Lillian and Helen, *The Players* (Simon & Schuster).

Stanislavsky, Constantin, *An Actor Prepares* (Theatre Arts).

Stanislavsky, Constantin, *Building a Character* (Theatre Arts).

Stanislavsky, Constantin, *Creating a Role* (Theatre Arts).

Stanislavsky, Constantin, *My Life in Art* (Theatre Arts).

Turner, Clifford, *Voice and Speech in the Theatre* (Pitman).

3) Choosing the Play

What to look for in a good script, how to find the right play for a specific group.

Many amateur drama groups fall down in their choice of play. The world over, they are persistently guilty of choosing material far beyond them. It invariably transpires that they have neither the director, the backstage crew, the designers nor the actors to present the play with any degree of proficiency. Hence good plays are done very badly and sometimes bad plays very badly, which may be considered even worse! A play must be selected carefully and there are several factors to be taken into account when doing this. Surely, the first considerations should be: "Is this play worth doing? Is it worth the energy and the expense?"

Then we have to face other highly controversial questions: "What is a good play? How can we be sure that the play we have chosen will be widely acclaimed?"

We can't know for sure, but we can apply simple tests. Before I accept a directing assignment I want to know:

Has the play got a worthwhile theme? The great masterpieces have a universal theme, and even the humblest little one-act play has a theme of some kind. Comedy, as well as tragedy, has a theme, and sometimes the underlying theme of a comedy is serious; it is only the treatment that is comic.

Has it got a good plot? Is there a good clear story, leading up to a climax? Is there enough conflict in the story to make it really dramatic?

Are the characters real people, and not just puppets? Are you interested in what happens to them?

Has the play good and vivid dialogue? Good dialogue must be easy to speak, selective, and heightened above ordinary speech, though not too literary.

Is the play well constructed? Is the exposition clear? Are there good "curtains" and does the play lead up well to its final curtain? Is the main plot clearly defined? Are all the characters essential?

Lastly, if the play is a comedy, is it really as funny as it appears at the first reading, or will the cast begin to tire of it after a few weeks' rehearsal?

You have to decide whether your first production is to be a programme of one-act plays, or a full-length play. If your actors have had no previous experience, you may prefer to present a programme of three one-act plays, which will make less demand on any one individual actor. But there is much more satisfaction in producing a three-act play, and it is preferred by the audience.

There is no doubt that the writing and characterization is usually of a much higher standard in a full-length play. This is partly because the length of a three-act play allows a character to be more fully developed, and partly because one-act plays are not a commercial proposition in the professional theatre, and few of the well-known playwrights are writing them.

There are, of course, exceptions. Shaw, Barrie, Galsworthy, Synge, Yeats, Pinter and Simpson are a few of the great British playwrights who have written one-act plays in their day. Some years ago, Noel Coward introduced a triple bill of one-act plays while, more recently, Terence Rattigan experimented by presenting two plays on one bill—*Playbill* and *Separate Tables.* There are also some excellent one-act plays by American writers, Edward Albee among them.

Never forget that members of your audience are paying for their seats and their tastes must be taken into consideration. You must not give an audience fed on musical comedy or the cinema an unrelieved diet of Greek tragedy or avant-garde theatre of the absurd.

A lot of amateur drama groups, however, will take no risks whatsoever when choosing their plays. Their excuses usually are: "Our audience won't understand it." or "Nothing highbrow. Our audience won't like it." Unless you've tried to present something new, how do you know? Audiences are not nearly so dim-witted as some actors believe. It is a good plan to present one of these so-called "highbrow" or "serious" plays now and again—as an experiment. Too many groups do nothing more than one Broadway success after another, which can sometimes be a mistake. Popular plays are seen by many people when they are performed professionally. These people may tend to compare your actors with the professionals they saw in the same parts.

There is also an argument, however, that popular plays are always acceptable—especially by residents of remote areas who rarely venture down to Toronto or New York. In the country it may be safe to present the Neil Simon repertoire of such thundering successes as *Barefoot in the Park, The Odd Couple* and *Come Blow Your Horn,* but by the same token it is safe to assume that the larger towns and cities have seen enough of these plays. They are now looking for new experiences in theatre, and the onus is upon enterprising groups to provide them.

A scene from a typical
melodrama: *The Milk
Train Doesn't Stop Here
Anymore.* Randolph
Rhodes

When you are sure that the play you have in mind is a good one, you must then decide whether it is within the range of your cast. Obviously, an all-women group should not choose a play with a predominantly male cast, nor a youth group one intended for middle-aged women. But what is less obvious is that your choice should not be beyond the imagination or technical skill of your group. Sophisticated modern comedy is not suitable for an unsophisticated village group which may utterly fail to comprehend the real people beneath the superficial exterior, and whose technical skill may not be capable of speaking dialogue, much of which is deliberately casual. When such plays are attempted, the result is usually a slow production with farcical characters and heavy dialogue, or the dialogue and characters may emerge as completely colourless. Youth clubs, too, sometimes tackle plays beyond their scope. I have seen that grim little masterpiece, *The Dear Departed,* by Stanley Houghton, played with such zest and charm that the whole play has come over as a rollicking farce. Yet from both village and youth groups, when playing within their capabilities, I have seen performances that far surpass many of those by the more affluent and sophisticated groups.

Sometimes, however, an adult play can be performed quite effectively by young people, provided it is one in which the characters are intentionally nondescript or secondary to the play's message. Suppose, for example, you were contemplating *Pygmalion,* you would have to look for people of the right age group, otherwise the conflicts would not stand up, the class-conscious aspect would fall apart, the man-woman relationships would never materialize and, in short, the great work would split down the middle and lose many of the things Shaw had hoped to say when he wrote it. On the other hand, there are plays written in which what the characters have to say is more important than who they are. Most of these fall into the category of the theatre of the absurd, a branch of theatre in which the playwright makes important commentaries through absurd situations.

Thornton Wilder's *Our Town* is very much a message play that can be performed by young actors. So too are some of Edward Albee's one-act plays, including *The Sandbox* and *Zoo Story.* Strange as it may seem, some scenes from Shakespeare can also be effectively handled by young adults—such as the last act of *A*

Midsummer Night's Dream and moments in *Romeo and Juliet.*

Lucille Fletcher's *Sorry, Wrong Number,* can be performed by young people, too. It tells of a crippled woman's plight in trying to contact her husband by telephone. He is working late. She is alone. The woman makes several telephone calls from her sickbed, gets a series of wrong numbers and that night is accidentally plugged into a conversation between two men planning to commit a murder. She later talks to a member of the New York Police Department who refuses to believe her story about the planned murder. Finally, as she is asking her local hospital to send her round a nurse because she's nervous, she hears footsteps coming up the stairs. She is ironically murdered by one of the men she'd heard earlier—discussing the crime.

As you will imagine, the play depends almost entirely on the amount of tension the woman and those actors in several smaller roles can generate. If young people were able to produce just this, it could compensate for their being too young for the roles.

In Canada, the problem of finding the right play is compounded. Many groups have a mixture of English and North American voices and they frequently ask, "In what plays can we safely utilize our forces?" This is a sensible question and I wish it were asked more often. An Englishman in a Neil Simon comedy sounds as ridiculous as a North American trying to portray a character from Noel Coward. In each case, the dialogue has been written in an idiom. Although an American may be able to learn an Englishman's lines (and vice versa), his dialogue will not run so smoothly and authentically from the tongue as it would if the Englishman and the American were playing their own parts.

Without question, the best plays in which English and North American voices can be put together are those that are either historical, make universal statements, or have nondescript settings. An example is Jean Paul Sartre's *No Exit,* a searing one-act drama in which three people are made to spend the entire play in one room, which, it transpires, is the author's metaphysical hell. What Sartre says in his play is far more important than the nationality of his characters. Actually, two are supposed to be French; the third is Spanish. But the play functions well on the three levels I have mentioned. It is historical, makes a political, universal statement and could have been set in a room anywhere in the world.

Similarly, the rule applies to Greek tragedies and plays like Fay and Michael Kanin's *Rashomon,* which is set in Japan with a cast made up solely of Orientals.

Other plays suitable for mixed voices include those by Shakespeare and many of the well-known European playwrights such as Brecht, Genêt, Ionesco, Chekhov and Strindberg. In the case of the European works, the suitability should be especially obvious. Since they cannot be presented this side of the Atlantic in their original languages any objection to their being performed with a combination of North American and English voices would be ludicrous.

Groups should always cast an eye to the future and be looking constantly—perhaps through a specifically-appointed play-reading committee—for new works to perform. In so doing, they must never ignore the playwright in their midst. Groups will need him just as he will need groups.

Reading List

Cole, Toby, Ed., *Playwrights on Playwrighting* (Hill and Wang).
Gassner, John, *Masters of the Drama* (Dover).
Gassner, John, *The Theatre in our Times* (Crown).
Goodman, Ralph, Ed., *Drama on Stage* (Holt, Rinehart and Winston).
Hunt, Hugh, *The Live Theatre* (Oxford).
MacCowan and Melnitz, *The Living Stage* (Prentice-Hall).
Nicoll, Allardyce, *British Drama* (Harrap).
Nicoll, Allardyce, *The Development of the Theatre* (Harrap).
Nicoll, Allardyce, *The Theatre and Dramatic Theory* (Harrap).
Seyler, Athene and Haggard, Stephen, *The Craft of Comedy* (Muller).
Southern, Richard, *The Seven Ages of the Theatre* (Hill and Wang).

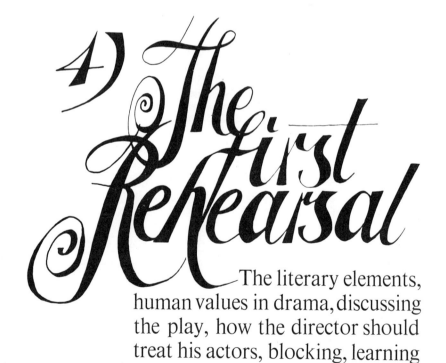

4) The First Rehearsal

The literary elements, human values in drama, discussing the play, how the director should treat his actors, blocking, learning lines, masking, upstaging.

The average man in the street goes to see a play or a movie simply to be entertained. He either likes what he sees, dislikes it or remains indifferent. Usually he doesn't know why he feels the way he does and can't therefore support his verdict. People involved in the theatre, however, especially the actors and directors, should be able to go a step further. They should be able to assume for the moment the role of a drama critic and say *why* a production succeeded or failed.

Of course, there are as many reasons why a play can collapse as there are types of theatre. A farce, for instance, can flop (and usually does in amateur theatre) because the characters have not remained real people in the unlikely situation invented by the author. Perhaps they've tended to "clown," and because of it the farce has ended up being played as a broad, relatively unsophisticated comedy. Perhaps in a piece of theatre of the absurd the cast has not spoken every absurd word as though each has utterly believed it. Perhaps a melodrama, a simple drawing-room comedy or an historical play has lacked its own particular style—one of the most common deficiencies in amateur productions and one which is usually brought about through shoddy, shortsighted casting. Generally, however, many of the common faults in the Little Theatre could be eliminated if the director and his cast met before the play was given its movement, specifically to analyse the script.

Before blocking the play, the actors and the director have to agree on several major aspects. These include the kind of vehicle they are about to rehearse, what it sets out to say, how it says it, the strengths and types of relationships amongst its characters, which character has lines that embrace the philosophy of the play, where they come, what and where are the climaxes, and a host of other points. In brief, every actor has to know how his character fits into the plot. When I'm directing amateurs in a play, I make sure they know how other people fit in too. To help them see this, I talk about the basic elements of good literature. I point them out in the script—the fate, the coincidence, the chance, the irony. Then I explain what I call "the treatments" or "the tools" by which a writer makes his work both vital and interesting—such things as conflict, the macabre, satire and pathetic fallacy. It takes extra time to diagnose these elements and note how they are applied, but experience shows the effort to be extremely worthwhile. Not only does it give the play its dimension, but it serves to prove the importance of script analysis for future productions.

A good actor and a good director must both know that even some of the most serious plays have splashes of satire. Since it is generally accepted that satire is a humorous criticism or a ridiculing of something or someone normally taken seriously, these moments might have to be accentuated for comic relief. Of course, moments of comic relief are not always satirical. They can merely be funny lines written to break or build tension. If the play is to be kept in perspective—especially if it's a black comedy where humour is secondary to pathos—then the values and treatment of these comic lines have to be carefully assessed.

Humorous lines specifically written to ease tension, incidentally, are a trait of the comedy-suspense. An example provides a climax in Jack Weinstock's *Catch Me If You Can.* A young executive spends three anxious acts waiting nervously for the return of his missing wife. Whenever there is a knock on the door, the audience is made to feel, by a clever process of suspense writing, that she has returned. "Oh my God! " says the executive, drawing open the door to reveal instead the sombre, hatless figure of the family priest. "No," says the priest, "just one of his helpers."

I suppose the hatless priest standing in the doorway, poker-faced and with his hat upon his breast, presents a mild form of the macabre. On first sight, the audience thinks he has come to say that the missing wife has been found dead, and that he is there to make funeral arrangements. There's also an element of satire in the flippant manner in which he goes about his work, thus holding up the general conception of the Roman Catholic priest to gentle ridicule. The actor playing the priest in this play would be better able to carve a satirical character out of his role if he were told that he held satirical ammunition in what he said and did. Left to his own devices, his performance could become colourless, depriving the play of much of its humour.

There are many more obvious examples of the satirical and the macabre. Shakespeare's Romeo and Juliet die a macabre death, and it could be argued that all death is macabre. But Shakespeare uses his weapon to a much greater dramatic effect. He makes the star-crossed lovers die in one of the most macabre places—the vault in which Juliet has been laid to sleep off the effects of the drug given to her by the friar. At this point, of course, Juliet has already been given a funeral, even though she is still alive, which presents a touch of ironic gruesomeness. The play ends ironically with Romeo killing himself not knowing that his young bride is still alive, and Juliet deciding that life without Romeo is pointless, and stabbing herself. Not until the two lovers are dead do the conflicting families come together.

Pathetic fallacy, of particular importance in theatre since it sometimes involves sound and lighting effects, occurs where an author uses the elements of nature to heighten the drama or add to the irony of a situation. It takes a thunderstorm in the Rodgers and Hammerstein musical *The Sound of Music* to make the Von Trapp children, having agreed among themselves not to cooperate with their new governess, Maria Rainer, to finally realize that they need her. As the storm rages, one night, they seek protection in Maria's bedroom, where together they sing "The Lonely Goatherd." Verdi uses the technique effectively in the last act of his opera *Rigoletto.* A storm is welling up as Rigoletto, the hunchbacked court jester hires an assassin to kill the Duke for seducing his daughter, Gilda. The storm reaches a climax as Gilda, dressed as a young man, is mistaken for someone else and stabbed. She later dies her ironic death in the arms of her weeping father.

The director should meet his cast only with prerehearsal work done, otherwise he might not be able to answer questions from his actors, and if the group is a lively one there should be many of them. He will have his own ideas when discussing the play, but he should always be open to suggestions and be ready to listen to the opinions of others. He should encourage his actors to use their imaginations in the way they see and interpret their characters. If both the director and the actors are interpreting correctly, there is unlikely to be much divergence of opinion. If, however, there is, the director's ruling must be accepted since he sees the play as a whole, whereas the actor is primarily concerned with the part he is playing and his view may be out of focus. A thorough discussion on the elements, "weapons," and human values of the play will reveal any conflicts of opinion early. This will give the director time to smooth them out. Unfortunately, not enough amateur drama groups undertake sufficient preparatory work of this kind and their productions are the poorer for it.

The actors should come to their next rehearsals armed with pencils so they can write down their blocking as it is given them by the director. Some directors do not plan their blocking in advance. They prefer to rely upon the inspiration of the moment to make it a live interpretation. This method is rarely successful with amateurs. The director who appears to have everything, including his blocking, preplanned, inspires his cast with confidence. There is nothing worse than a director who is constantly changing his mind.

Actors can save themselves time and trouble by using initials for stage directions:

X.U.R.—cross up right
Sit D.S. Chesterfield—sit on downstage end of chesterfield
M.D.L.—move down left

When there are a number of chairs on the stage I prefer to number them for easy reference.

Stage directions are always given from the point of view of the actor. The right-hand side of the stage is therefore taken to mean the actor's right. The middle of the stage is centre (C), the back of the stage farthest from the audience is referred to as "up," and the portion

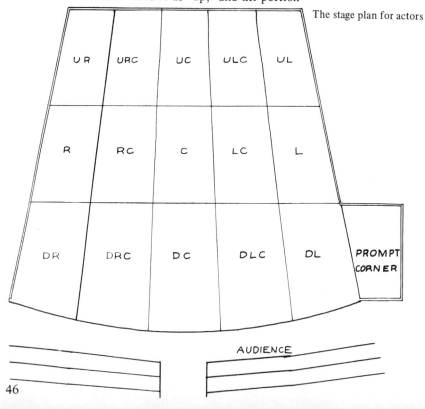

The stage plan for actors

nearest the front edge of the stage as "down." The prompter usually sits on the left-hand side, which is sometimes referred to as the prompt side, while the right-hand side may be called "O.P."—opposite prompt.

The director should not expect too much from his actors during these early blocking rehearsals. He should be content to see that they write down their moves correctly. If he bothers them with interpretation they will be confused and forget where to go on the rehearsal set. These early rehearsals are not very exciting but it's important to deal with the mechanics of the play before passing onto character development, the development of relationships and interpretation.

As the actors are being given their moves, the script assistant should be recording them in her prompt book so that she will be equipped to take blocking rehearsals should the director be taken ill. If a three-act play is being done, it is advisable, in order to consolidate the blocking, to go over each act several times before passing onto the next.

I know it is difficult for some groups to meet more than two or three times a week, but it's better to rehearse intensively over a short period rather than to spread rehearsals over too long a time. The trouble with most amateur productions is not that they are over-rehearsed—indeed many of them are woefully under-rehearsed—but that they are rehearsed for too long.

One play I directed in my amateur days was rehearsed once a week for five months. During that time, everyone of the nineteen parts was recast, some as many as four times, and we ended up with a completely different set of actors from those with whom we started out. The time factor was the chief reason for the ill luck of this play. With the best of intentions people accepted parts, only to find later that for personal reasons they could not carry on.

If the rehearsal time is short this is less likely to happen, and if necessary the actors should be prepared to make some sacrifices of leisure in order that the play be well done. A three-act play needs at least twenty-four three-hour rehearsals and a one-act play eight to ten rehearsals. The ideal period for a three-act play is two months, rehearsing twice a week the first two weeks, three times a week for the next month, and every night for the last two weeks.

The director must be quite firm about books being discarded within a certain time, for in every group there

These are rehearsal pictures of Neil Simon's *Plaza Suite,* directed in Montreal by the author. The director has insisted on his actors using props and important costumes early in rehearsal stage. Those familiar with the play will note the sensible casting. Davis Photography.

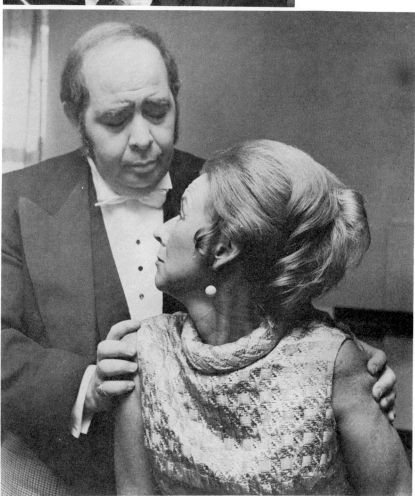

are people who have to be bullied into learning their lines. I insist that my players discard their books three weeks after rehearsals begin, and certainly not later than halfway through rehearsals. Until lines are learnt the actors cannot fully interpret the characters. Beginners often clutch their books long after they know their lines, because they don't know what to do with their hands, and when the book is wrenched from them they cling to the backs of chairs or other furniture.

It is unlikely that the actors will see the actual sets until just before the dress rehearsal, and sometimes not even until that day, but the director should explain in great detail to the actors the settings he envisages. He must obtain the correct dimensions of the stage on which the play is to be performed and mark out on his floor the exact size, using chairs to indicate door and window exits, and placing his furniture in exactly the same position every time. There is nothing more disconcerting than for the director to find that because he has been rehearsing on too large a floor space, his beautifully significant grouping has merged into one large crowd, or for the actor to find that the cup of tea, which in rehearsal he had only to stretch out his hand to receive, is now a yard from his grasp.

As soon as books are discarded the actors must begin to rehearse with properties. This is particularly important where a large number of properties are used, or where meals are eaten on stage. The timing of stage business is tricky and I have often seen the action of a play held up for several seconds because properties not used in rehearsals took longer to handle than was anticipated. The director must give the actor definite cues at which to do certain stage business, otherwise the actor may find that he has completed the job five minutes too soon and has nothing to do for the rest of the scene; or else has not half laid the table by the time the meal has to be eaten.

Groups with their own wardrobe departments work to great advantage because costumes worn in rehearsal will feel like real clothes and not fancy dress in performance. Amateurs tend to forget that clothes worn on stage must look as though they have been worn many times before and are not new. Having travelled through wind and rain, an actor should not appear on stage looking like a dummy from the window of a men's outfitter. His clothes and hair should bear traces of what he has just come through. Once I saw a production of *Hamlet* in which that seasoned campaigner Fortinbras arrived on the scene immaculately clad in satin and without even a speck of mud on his boots or apparel.

The actual process of moving actors around on stage is complex and tiring, and requires the patience of a cart horse. Again, there are many books to be read on the subject, but in the final analysis much of what a director envisages has to be felt by the performer. He might say, for instance, move from A to B. If he is a good director he will explain the motivation with which the move must be made. The actor has to agree with the motivation in order to properly execute the move. It may mean his having to break the move slightly, or be caught mid-step, in his reaction to a very important line. An example of such a motivated hiatus in movement can be seen in Edward Albee's *Who's Afraid of Virginia Woolf?* It is well after 2 a.m. and George and his wife Martha are arguing in their living room. Martha says, "Make me a drink." George mutters, "What?" and Martha repeats her request: "I said, make me a drink." At this, George replies, "Well, I don't suppose a night-cap'd kill either one of us," and rises. Martha's next line is delivered as her husband makes for the bar: "A night-cap! Are you kidding? " she says. "We've got guests coming over."

It is 2 a.m., remember, and George has already told of his weariness. Under these circumstances, he could hardly brush off the next line lightly. To show his disapproval of his wife's plan to have people in well past bedtime, his next line should be accentuated. When I directed the play I punctuated George's line with a hiatus. He stopped in mid-stride and said, "Guests. Guests. We've got guests coming over." George then turned to face Martha, there was a pause, the pace quick-ened and George continued his dialogue with a com-pletely different attitude: "Good Lord, Martha. Don't you know what time it is?"

This is a very obvious situation, but even obvious situations seem to be overlooked in amateur blocking. For a play to be successful, movement does not have to be brilliant—just sensible. Straight lines should be avoid-ed at all cost, unless the scene calls for a parade of soldiers, and directors should learn some of the many other effective "tricks" of synchronizing blocking with dialogue, by reading books written specifically on the subject.

Among these tricks there is one of the most

common, yet one of the most neglected. If an actor speaks, and then moves, the move is accentuated. If he moves, and then speaks, the attention falls upon the dialogue. If he does the two together, then both get the same amount of emphasis. This means that if one of my actors ever had such a line, "Get out of my life, I hate you," I would have him move, stop, and then deliver the line, to give it maximum impact. If he delivered the line while he was moving, it would not add up to very much and the chances are that the audience would not believe it. Of course, I could play the move the other way. A temperamental woman might make a dramatic exit out of the line by facing squarely the person to whom she was directing it (one of the best visual methods of creating conflict), delivering it tersely, and then making a dash for the door. Whether or not this method had its right impact would depend on how she moved away.

Directors should always be careful not to have all their actors facing front at one given time. It must be remembered that moments in a play have focal points and by having faces staring straight out means that, for that moment, the focal point is gone. If two people are resolving a love affair at downstage right, it would be ludicrous to have everyone else looking out to see how many empty seats there were in the theatre auditorium. A sensible director would use all other people on stage to build this glorious moment in the script by having them look on with appropriate attitudes, even to the point of having some characters in profile.

I like profiles on stage. I also like to see people's backs. It is wrong to think that a back is dull. To the contrary, a back can be very telling. Supposing the curtain went up on seven actors and one was upstage, with his back to the audience, looking out of a window, which character do you think the audience would see first? I am sure they would see the one who was different from the others and ask themselves, "Why is that man looking through the window?"

One would have to suppose, however, that to justify the view of the actor's back in this case, his looking out of the window was so important that it had to be accentuated.

Actors should be aware that moves can point up dialogue better than anything else and they should try to employ this technique without having to be told by a director. For example:

Man: Is it to be assumed that you love me no more?
Woman: Yes

Imagine this woman putting her cup down on the word "Yes." You'd be surprised at how much one word can be driven uncompromisingly into an audience by one simple movement. Of course, if the woman wanted to be less dramatic and more flippant about her reply, she could deliver the "Yes" while bringing the cup to her lips. It would depend on what the director wanted and what line the actress felt her character would take under the circumstances. This brings us back to that all-important pre-rehearsal analysis of the play.

A scene from *Sailor Beware!* Note the ragged grouping and lack of focal point. An actor is "masked" behind the sailor.

While actors are being blocked into a play, they should be aware of the many aspects that spoil the visual effect. Masking always looks shoddy. Upstaging a colleague (stealing the audience's attention from him at one of his important moments by causing him to speak upstage) is a trait of the selfish, inconsiderate, unintelligent actor. Standing for too long behind furniture, when the situation can be rectified by a simple move of a few inches, does not compliment the eye. Directors should watch for these points from the first rehearsal, so they do not become imprinted into what the audience will eventually see.

Reading List
Gielgud, John, *Stage Directions* (Heinemann).

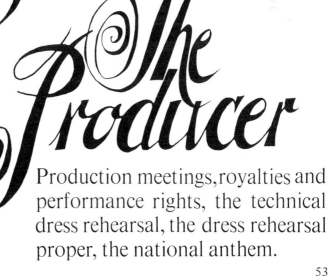

5) The Producer

Production meetings, royalties and performance rights, the technical dress rehearsal, the dress rehearsal proper, the national anthem.

While the director has been rehearsing diligently with his actors, the backstage personnel should have been meeting regularly under the chairmanship of the producer. This leader is to a play what a publisher is to a book. Although he has nothing to do with the interpretation of the production, the producer's job is every bit as important as that of the director's. Indeed, it is unlikely that one could function without the other. Producers can't direct plays and directors can't always produce them because the jobs call for two different types of individual.

Just as the director is to blame if the play fails on the performance level, the producer is at fault if the lighting, sound, make-up, properties, front-of-house and box-office arrangements are not properly executed, because he oversees them all. He's also in charge of the financial arrangements of a production (paying royalties and seeing that materials for such items as set building and costumes are paid for), and therefore he has to keep in close contact with the treasurer. In brief, he must be a businessman-watchdog who takes the production management off the shoulders of the director, thereby allowing him to spend as much time as he possibly can on artistic interpretation.

Like the director, the producer is usually chosen by a group's executive. The choice is not always an easy one because besides needing all the necessary qualities and administrative experience, the producer must have a personality which enables him to establish a solid working relationship with the director. If a director and a producer did not get on well together, a large, irreparable gap could develop in the organization and possibly not reveal itself until the play reached the audience.

Generally speaking, the producer and the director choose their backstage personnel together. However, other than selecting my own set designer (or musical director if I'm staging a musical), I leave the job to my business partner. He invariably knows more people in his group and, more important, knows those upon whom we can safely rely. I contend that as a director I have enough pre-production work to accomplish without having time to interfere with a job that can be performed just as well, if not better, by someone else. Besides, one of the biggest traps that awaits a director is that of making people who work backstage feel superfluous. It's difficult enough getting hard work from backstage hands, who are rarely acclaimed by an audience, without compounding the problem by making them feel unwanted and insignificant. Suffice it to say that a good director never interferes with someone else's job unless it is not being done properly, in which case the producer is left to find a replacement.

Although the director and the producer may frequently get together at odd moments during rehearsals, most of their collaborating should be done at specifically arranged production meetings attended by everyone heading a backstage department. At these meetings, the producer may be asked to answer an assortment of questions which could range from, "Where can we rent a tape recorder?" and "Who stole the tool kit?" to "How much are we charging this year for tickets?" and "How much can we spend on wigs and paint?" The director might want to discuss the lighting and sound, or even ask the treasurer (through the producer) if extra money is available for buying new equipment. The discussion could then move to the front-of-house area of the theatre. Are latecomers to be admitted? Who's in charge of the cloakroom this year? Who's handing out the programmes? There should always be a great deal to discuss at a production meeting.

The producer's first job, however, is a very important one, although it is sometimes forgotten. Even before the choice of play has been finalized, he must find out whether it is available for performance by amateurs. He must also find out the royalty cost. I cannot stress this enough. One Little Theatre group in the Maritimes was fined $200 for failing to meet the royalty of Samuel Beckett's one-act play, *Endgame.* Another more experienced group actually ventured into production with *The Show-Off,* and, after the play had been cast and the group had spent money hiring costumes, was told that the amateur performing rights were not yet available. With more foresight, the producer could have saved valuable time and money.

Performing rights are a form of licence and must always be obtained from the holder of the copyright *before* the play can legally be performed. Not only is it an infringement of copyright to perform a copyright play without the consent of the author or his agent, but it is also an infringement to alter a play in any way, to make scripts of it for rehearsals from the published edition, or to reprint in any form either the whole or part of it. Producers should familiarize themselves with such regulations.

Copyright in most parts of the world, including North America, exists during the lifetime of the author and for fifty years after his death. In the event of a play being performed posthumously, copyright exists for fifty years after the date of the first performance. In the case of old plays which have been adapted, and foreign plays which have been translated, the adapter is the owner of the copyright in the first instance, and the translator and the author jointly in the second.

At the time of applying for performing rights, the producer should ascertain the royalty cost. This can vary by thirty dollars or more per performance. Groups can expect to pay between twenty and fifty dollars a night for a three-act play. A one-act play can cost between five and fifteen dollars, depending on its popularity and its author. Professional theatre companies are charged more so amateur producers must make sure they are paying the correct scale, and find out whether they can receive a special concession on the basis of the number of performances they intend giving.

A royalty fee should never be begrudged because it is the way in which the author receives payment for his work. Since the rehearsal and performance of the play will have given the actors, and ultimately the audience, much pleasure, the payment to the author of his just due should be the first consideration This applies equally to performances for charity and to those where no charge is made for admission. When plays are presented for charity, groups sometimes expect to be allowed to perform them without paying a fee, but they forget that authors probably contribute to various benevolent causes of their own and cannot be counted on to assist others. In any case, the right to forego his fee does not always rest with the author. Quite often it is up to his publisher or agent.

Authors' agents and publishers frequently forego royalties on private performances, but there is no clear definition of what exactly is a "private" performance. The publisher Samuel French defines a private performance thus:

A performance given in a school or college, the audience consisting solely of the members of the school, resident staff, and a maximum of fifty relatives or friends, provided no money or consideration is taken for admission, no programmes sold, nor a collection made
A performance given in a hospital to in-patients and

resident members of the staff
A performance given in an institution, to old people and
staff residing on the premises

In these cases no acting fee would be charged, but in every instance it is absolutely essential to obtain the consent of the author or his agent—even before giving a private performance.

Usually, royalty details are explained in the front of the acting edition. Where this is not the case the onus is upon the producer to find out. Under no circumstances should it be assumed that, because royalties have not been mentioned in the script, the play can be performed without a fee. And here's another word of warning: don't assume that a published play is necessarily available to amateurs. Sometimes performing rights are withdrawn when a professional touring company is due, as two productions of the same play in the same area could hurt business either way.

It can be seen that the producer has a mundane kind of job which few people seem to want but which is of vital importance to the success of the production. When I directed the Rodgers and Hammerstein musical *The Sound of Music,* a clause was written into my contract giving the producer the power to make final decisions in the event of any dispute I might have with such persons as the musical director, choral director or set designer. In effect, then, the producer becomes a kind of labour relations man, a mediator.

To bring the work of his backstage crew into view, let's imagine it is now a few days before opening night, production meetings have gone smoothly, and it's time for the first of two dress rehearsals. Groups having to hire a hall for their performances may find three dress rehearsals too expensive. They should, however, try to arrange two. It is safe to predict that they will need them both.

The first rehearsal must be geared to the technical aspects of the production—sound, lighting and scene changing cues. It should be preceded by a costume parade so that the director can see how costumes will look under lighting and against the colours of the sets. The setting up of scenery takes time, lights may have to be adjusted, and the level of sound effects established. There's not always time for a complete performance of the play, which can sometimes be frustrating for the actors who are left to wait around in costume. However, they should realize that the production depends in a sense on the worst technician, and should view the proceedings with patience and understanding.

Any technical changes can be made for the final dress rehearsal—the dress rehearsal proper—which must be a complete run-through of the play. As the final co-ordination of the vocal, the visual and everything technical, it must take the form of a preview of the play as the audience will eventually see it, even down to the speed at'which the curtains open and close upon each act, and the speed at which the house lights dim. The rehearsal should be run with correctly-timed inter-missions (usually of ten minutes each) so that actors will know exactly how long they've got to negotiate any costume or make-up changes. I also like to time my dress rehearsals to satisfy myself that the show will not drag when it gets before the audience.

By the start of the final dress rehearsal, if the actors have arrived early, donned their costumes, been made-up and familiarized themselves with the set, they should have mastered the opening of doors and windows and adjusted themselves to their new acting space. However much a director tries to see that the acting space in the rehearsal hall will coincide with that on the set, his actors are usually surprised by their new environ-ment. A door might be a foot farther upstage than it was when the set was defined with chairs; a window might be farther downstage. Without disrupting backstage personnel who might still be working on the set around them, actors should use the first dress rehearsal and spare moments during the second to practise their entrances and exits. They should also go over move-ments that may call for precision—like vaulting over the chesterfield or diving through the window!

The director and the producer sit together at the back of the theatre for the second dress rehearsal, watch-ing their show closely and stopping it only under very extreme circumstances. It's most unnerving for a cast to face opening night not having had the satisfaction of a smoothly-flowing dress rehearsal. So the director is now concerned with building up spirits—even if things do go wrong—rather than breaking them down. He should take notes only of glaring faults and deliver them quickly to his actors after the rehearsal. Many accidents that occur on stage do so only once. An actor who drops a cup at dress rehearsal isn't necessarily going to do it on opening night, so the chances of my noting an incident such as this at a dress rehearsal are remote. I concern myself more with such items as insecure scenery, bad lighting and sound cues, inaudibility of actors, and offstage noises by members of the cast waiting to make their entrances.

Incidentally, at both dress rehearsals it's imperative to practise the curtain calls two or three times, and to go over the music that is being used either before the show, after it or during intermission. This is especially important if music on records is being used rather than music that has been taped. Record companies sometimes make mistakes in their labelling. A friend of mine bought a record of "God Save the Queen" and played it for the first time after a performance on opening night. "God Save the Queen" turned out to be "Rule Britannia." Thinking that he must have put the wrong side on, my friend picked up the record, examined it and replaced it on the turntable, making sure that "God Save The Queen" was uppermost. Alas, the record played "Rule Britannia" again!

Actually, I think my friend was wrong in wanting his national anthem at the end of the play because it probably broke the post-performance atmosphere. If the national anthem is to be used (and bylaws in some towns and cities stipulate that it must be played at *every* public performance), then it should occur at the beginning to tell the audience the play is about to start. I know of no better way of getting people to their seats!

Reading List
Gassner, John, *Producing the Play* (Dryden).
Plummer, Gail, *The Business of Show Business* (Harper).

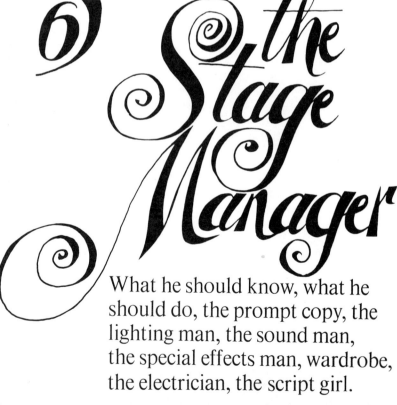

6) the Stage Manager

What he should know, what he
should do, the prompt copy, the
lighting man, the sound man,
the special effects man, wardrobe,
the electrician, the script girl.

Even though it is a most integral part of a production in performance, the position of stage manager has been subjected in the amateur theatre to a ludicrous lack of definition. Many Little Theatre groups tend to look upon it as a general backstage dog's-body job that no one wants, hence far too often the stage manager arrives reluctantly at the dress rehearsal to hammer nails in the set, help fix the lights, or make the coffee. I've even known a stage manager to present himself for the first time at the dress rehearsal and be completely unknown to the actors, which suggests that he didn't know when and where his work was supposed to have begun. He was unaware, for instance, that the stage manager has preparatory work (like the director, the actors and the producer), and that the ultimate technical success of the production hangs almost exclusively on how diligently this work is accomplished.

Of course, he can still help out with mundane backstage chores, and often must, for keen, knowledgeable stagehands are almost as hard to find in amateur theatre as Hamlets. However, he should never forget that his is a specialized backstage position which, depending on the size and intricacy of the production, often demands impeccable precision. Indeed, far from being unwanted, the job of stage manager should be highly coveted, because it is usually immensely interesting and satisfying.

Although his name suggests that he's there to merely "manage the stage," the stage manager's first consideration should be how to take over from the director and maintain complete artistic control. You can't steer a ship without first studying its course and, in much the same way, in order to gain this control, the good stage manager studies the play and begins his work with the birth of the production—when it's being cast, analysed and blocked. He must attend as many rehearsals as he possibly can to find out not only what the play is about but, more important still, how the director is treating it. In the final analysis, while the director is responsible for *what* happens on stage, the stage manager, the first-class unobtrusive organizer able to foresee the inevitable pitfalls of theatre before they become insurmountable, is concerned with *how* it happens on stage.

To do this job well, he must have an excellent memory and be tactful, practical, unfailingly cheerful, calm and, above all, even-tempered with a special liking for working with people. While the director and his actors may occasionally throw a tantrum, the stage manager cannot afford to indulge in such a luxury. Any display of temper on his part, especially during a performance, could manifest itself in a backstage blunder seen by the audience. He must concern himself wholeheartedly with clearing the way for the actors to portray their roles in a minimum of confusion.

Apart from ensuring that the backstage area is kept clean, clear and quiet, and setting up a system by which the actors are called in plenty of time for their entrances, the stage manager is responsible for controlling the lighting, sound and special effects cues. This is a job which demands a good rhythmic sense if these cues are to complement the movements of the actors, or help create the mood of the scene, or both.

However, as important as it is, a good sense of rhythm can be superfluous unless the stage manager has prepared in *meticulous detail* his most important document. This is called the prompt copy of the script and is the stage manager's complete guide to what happens, when, where, how, why, who and what's involved. The veritable Bible of the production, it could be likened, I suppose, to a gourmet's cookbook, except that if a gourmet loses his cookbook he can quietly and privately improvise, whereas the stage manager, even with his good memory, can improvise without his prompt copy but only at the extremely high risk of making mistakes that will be seen by the audience. Indeed, so important is the prompt copy that it must be very carefully prepared to include every move the actors make, cues for lighting, sound and special effects (smoke or shadows, for instance), and any make-up or costume changes, quick or otherwise.

The prompt copy has to contain so much information that it is impossible to write it all in the margin of the acting edition of the script. The script has to undergo rather cruel treatment. Its pages must be taken out and placed between the blank pages of a hardbound exercise book. If a tight budget decrees that the stage manager can only have one script then he will have to make sure that both sides of his script pages are accessible, by making a firm fold down the inside margin and sticking it to the blank pages in the exercise book. If two scripts are available, however, the complete page may be stuck down. This obviously makes a firmer prompt copy, and firm it must be. Remember, it has to undergo persistent handling throughout rehearsals and performances.

The stage manager can begin underlining some of the obvious cues (doorbells, lights, actors' entrances and exits, and music) that may already be specified in the script, and may add any others as rehearsals progress. He must also find suitable moments in the script when warnings of cues can be given. Warnings are usually given about half a page before the actual cue. So you will understand that the prompt copy will have such markings in it as:

WARN	Doorbell
GO	Doorbell
ENTER	John
WARN	Blackout
ENTER	Bill
GO	Blackout

For easy reference, the stage manager should number all his cues and consider marking them down in his prompt copy in different colours—blue pencil for sound, red for light, green for music and so on.

Additionally the stage manager's pre-performance work includes the preparation of certain lists known as plot sheets—itemized scene-by-scene accounts of costumes, furniture, sound effects, lights, properties, music and scenery, as and when they are required in the play. Since many of these items may have to be either bought, borrowed, stolen, hired or made, the experienced stage manager begins compiling his plot sheets early. When he hands them out to his departmental heads they in turn have plenty of time in which to meet the production's technical requisites, thus avoiding last-minute pressures. Since any extra items he may need will have to be included in the play's budget he must, needless to say, attend all production meetings.

Even when he's satisfied that both his prompt copy and plot sheets are complete, the stage manager should continue to attend rehearsals in case the director has made changes. He has to be completely up-to-date at all times. The director might decide he wants one of the characters dressed in purple instead of red, and that the chesterfield in act three is to be replaced by two rocking chairs. He might also decide to cut out parts of the dialogue and, in so doing, shorten the amount of time between light and sound cues and generally throw the

63

prompt copy out of perspective.

The most ironical aspect of stage management is that, broadly speaking, when it is done well and with the fullest impact, the audience doesn't notice it. That is to say that a critic or an adjudicator often only becomes aware of stage management when it is sloppy or, alternatively, when it's of a highly intricate nature in a production known to be particularly difficult. The stage manager will then draw rare and well-deserved praise.

Some small groups try to combine the job of the stage manager and the producer but this is a mistake. The two jobs are totally different and both are full-time. The result of the combination is that neither is done well. I recommend a most diligent search for an efficient stage manager. When found he should be encouraged and given a free hand. The wise director and producer will not interfere with backstage arrangements during performances. They will leave the entire running of the show to the stage manager.

As in the case of the director, the stage manager should not be chosen because he's willing, or because he's had the job for the past fifteen years. He should be chosen on the basis of his knowledge and ability to administer a situation at a time when nothing must go wrong. Of course, you could assume that a man who's done the job for fifteen years must have acquired some experience along the way. But what kind of experience? Have all his shows been well-managed from backstage? How serious have his mistakes been? Is he able to cope when something serious goes wrong?

Unquestionably, the good stage manager must have theatrical intuition. If something is about to go wrong on stage, he must be among the first to sense it and the first to find a quick solution. I remember experiencing a supreme example of the quick-thinking stage manager during a performance of *The Owl and the Pussycat,* starring Eartha Kitt, at the Royal Alexandra Theatre, Toronto. About halfway through the play, Miss Kitt had to climb into a cupboard. Immediately, the cupboard began to rock backwards and forwards. The stage manager plunged the theatre into complete darkness and no sooner had he done this when the cupboard fell onto the stage. In less than ten seconds it was returned to its normal position and the stage lights went up again—to the applause of an audience saluting the quick-thinking stage manager. The play went on as though nothing had happened. On another occasion, during a regional final of the annual Dominion Drama Festival at Hart House, University of Toronto, the stage manager saved an embarrassing situation during a scene which found a group of airmen playing darts. The stage lights went off just as the dartboard began its journey to the floor. By the time they went on again, the dartboard had been restored to its wall and the game was underway again.

Conversely, I still recall with embarrassment my last exit in a play in London, England, some years ago, when the scenery fell upon me and I stood for about half a minute (which seemed like hours) holding it up. The stage manager should have ordered the lights to be turned off to spare me the embarrassment of grappling with a ten-foot flat. Alas, I was left to put the flat back into position before the howling audience, and afterwards I went to tell the stage manager that his set was falling apart and needed some work before the next performance. He wasn't even watching the show. Instead he was drinking coffee with some of the actors in the dressing room.

Actors need their stage manager far more than their stage manager needs them. When he's not there, they are the first to feel his absence. The last time I badly wanted the stage manager was when the curtain became stuck at the end of Noel Coward's *Blithe Spirit.* I'd delivered Charles Condomine's last triumphant speech and had broken into the laughter that was supposed to have risen up to meet the curtain coming down. The curtain didn't move one inch. I had to stay there laughing for some time before the lighting man sensed something was wrong and blacked out the lights. "What happened? " I asked the stage manager afterwards. He replied, "We were trying to fix the curtain so you wouldn't have to stay out there too long."

If he needs administrative help, as well he might if the production is a particularly large one, the stage manager should not use just anyone backstage who happens to be free at the time. Instead he should appoint an assistant stage manager known as the A.S.M., and should apportion him jobs accordingly at the start of the production.

Let's now consider other people who work backstage under the stage manager. These vary according to the size of the group. Some small groups have an assistant stage manager, who combines the duties of "props," prompter, electrician and special effects person. Larger groups have a separate individual for each job, all of whom are responsible to the stage manager. Let us assume that there is one person for each job.

Script Assistant

The position of script assistant, or prompter, as it used to be called, is very important. But here again, it is often deprived of definition in amateur theatre and this, I think, accounts for its unpopularity. The typical Little Theatre script assistant (invariably a woman) tends to think that her job rests solely in helping the actors with their lines and blocking. When these have finally been learned, she sits at rehearsals with her head buried in her book, with nothing more to do than wait for someone to make a mistake, and make the coffee. Of course the job will be dull, if that's all she wants to do, but she could make it brighter by removing some of the emphasis from the prompting aspect of her work and concerning herself on a broader basis with helping not only the actors but the director as well. When I'm directing a large production I expect my script assistant to keep a thorough record of attendance (a job normally undertaken in the professional theatre by the stage manager) and conduct any extra rehearsals—without altering my blocking or interpretation—for actors having difficulty synchronizing their moves with their lines.

There is no doubt, however, that the script assistant's most gruelling work comes when the performers put down their scripts for the first time and are struggling for the next few rehearsals to remember both their lines and their moves. She will have copied the director's blocking carefully into her script, seeing that it corresponds at all times with the stage manager's prompt copy. She will also have noted all sound effects, and made arrangements for these to be incorporated into rehearsals so the actors can get used to hearing them.

Needless to say, as the production draws near, the script assistant will know the play almost as well as the director. This explains why one can combine the jobs of script assistant and stage manager, but only in small productions and in cases where the performers are sufficiently experienced so as not to want a prompter in the wings.

A good prompter must have a clear voice, a cool head and tact. Prompting should never occur during a dramatic pause; nothing infuriates an actor so much as this—even an actor who has been prompted persistently throughout the play. To guard against it, the prompter should mark the book whenever a dramatic pause occurs and not just rely upon memory. She should use common sense about prompting. During rehearsals she should take the actor back if he uses wrong words or twists phrases, but during a performance she should not interject unless he gives a wrong cue, or cuts so badly as to mislead a colleague. A sensitive prompter will learn from the expression on the actor's face whether he has "dried," and will give him the prompt swiftly before he has time to feel lost. A prompt should be delivered loudly so the actor can pick it up the first time.

In some professional theatres, it's the job of the script assistant or prompter, to give the special effects man his cues. In Little Theatre she can undertake some sound effects herself—telephones, front-door bells and door slams, for example—and thereby make her work during the performance more interesting.

Lighting Man (or Electrician)

There are two kinds of lighting man: one who has no knowledge of the theatre but plenty of knowledge about the equipment available, and one who knows a great deal about the theatre but who manipulates the lighting because no one else will do it. Somewhere in between is the happy balance. It's worthwhile making a concerted effort to find someone who is able to "feel" a light cue, rather than effect it mechanically. A good lighting man, having drawn up a lighting plot and had it approved by the stage manager and director at the beginning of a production, automatically knows where he should use a slow fade-out, as opposed to a sudden blackout, because he has a sense of theatre. He also knows that lighting is often only noticed by an audience when it is bad, or if it is tricky. That's why he draws up his lighting plot carefully and tries not to execute his cues too violently, unless otherwise wanted by the director.

A later chapter on backstage work shows how much there is to know about lighting.

Sound Man

There are two kinds of sound effects: those reproduced on a record or on a tape, and those reproduced manually. While I think the quality of sound effects records has improved vastly in recent years, I still feel that, whenever possible, it is more enterprising and often more effective to make these sounds manually.

The sound man is therefore often tested for ingenuity. Like his colleague, the lighting man, he should appreciate the different effects which can be accomplished by executing cues slowly on the one hand and harshly and quickly on the other.

A later chapter on backstage work deals more specifically with sound.

Wardrobe Mistress

The director and the wardrobe mistress should discuss costumes for each character. From then on, it's up to the wardrobe mistress to hire, borrow, steal, make or improvise. Of course, she should be a good needlewoman, but she should also have a solid sense of history, especially in so far as costumes are concerned. If I were looking for a wardrobe mistress, I'd try to engage an art teacher, who would have studied history anyway, and who would have a good eye for colour and shape.

A later chapter deals more specifically with costumes.

Property Master

By "props" we mean every article on the stage except the scenery and lighting equipment, and every article brought on by hand by an actor. The property master should also obtain the furniture. It's useful to have someone with a persuasive tongue who can charm Mrs. Jones into lending her best tea service, the local furniture store into lending a chesterfield or a table (in exchange for a free advertisement in the programme), or the flower shop into parting with the aspidistra in its window (in exchange for a free ticket for the show). If the property master is also a craftsman he will be able to make period pieces, which are sometimes difficult and expensive to hire.

Like the stage manager, he should evolve for himself an efficient system of ensuring that no property is forgotten on performance night. He will need a list for each scene of those that must be pre-set on stage and of those that are carried on by the actors.

It's a good idea to have hand props kept on a table in one spot offstage, left and right, so that they can be handed to the actor before his entry, and collected after his exit. Actors, by the way, are notorious for forgetting to return their properties, and a good property master is emphatic about keeping a scene-by-scene record of what is being used and what has yet to find its way back to the props table.

Reading List
Gruver, Bert, *Stage Manager's Handbook* (Harper).

the Play in Performance

Performance evaluation,
meeting the audience, curtain calls,
front-of-house, festivals.

The opening night arrives, all too quickly, it seems, and the play is about to be shown to the audience. The actors must be in their dressing rooms at least forty-five minutes before the performance begins, and the stage manager should have appointed one of his backstage staff to act as "call boy," with calls being made at half an hour and a quarter of an hour before curtain time.

The final call, however, is "Beginners, please!" with five minutes to go. Actors who appear early in the play must then go into the wings to await their entrances. The stage manager should be casting his eye around backstage to see that the lighting man, the sound man and the prompter are in their places. The overture music begins. At one minute before curtain time, the stage manager orders the stage lights on and the house lights down to three-quarters. With fifteen seconds to go, he should give the signal for the house lights to be completely faded out. The play is given a clean technical start if this coincides with the ending of the overture music.

The curtain goes up. The show is on.

Unless the theatre has to be used for other purposes between the time of the dress rehearsal and the

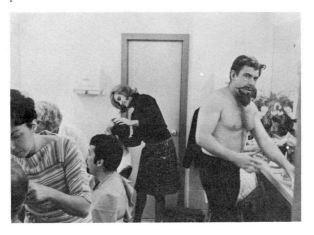

Tension rises in the dressing room. The opening performance is only minutes away.

performance, the stage manager should have left the stage ready. All he then has to do on opening night is check that everything is in order on the set and that properties are in their correct places offstage. It's too late to change anything now, so the director, having wished his cast well, consoled the nervous and expressed his confidence in his stage manager, goes to the back of the theatre and takes his seat in the audience. As much

71

as he may want to rush backstage and lend a helping hand if something goes wrong (and there's nearly always a production defect of some sort, although it usually passes unnoticed and is only magnified in the minds of those who have worked so closely with the play), he must stay seated and, so far as it's humanly possible, watch through the audience's eyes.

I say as far as humanly possible because it's not easy to remove yourself from within something that has involved your attention for so long and watch it from the outside as a stranger. Yet this is imperative if you are to learn something that can be applied to your next production. You must view your work as though you were your own worst enemy. A director who acquires nothing to pass on from show to show is a fool. If he's directed a failure he should know it, and admit it. But more than this, he should know *what* went wrong. Likewise, he should know not only that his play was a success, but *why*.

Through half-closed eyes, I subject my own productions in performance to the most careful scrutiny, asking such questions as the following:

Performance

Does the performance have an overall unity?
Is the meaning of the script projected?
Does the performance flow and have effective pacing?
Are the actors distinct and believable in their roles?
Have the play's climaxes been properly exploited and treated?
Is the production funny enough?
How much humour did I underestimate?
Does the performance have a spontaneous, "first time" quality about it?
Does it build towards the end?
What could I have done to improve the performance level?

Staging

Does the blocking contain any unmotivated movement?
Does the blocking complement the climaxes?
Do the lighting, costumes, sound and set add to the performance, or do they detract from it?
Is my staging imaginative?
What could I have done to improve the staging?

Script Evaluation

Does the script evoke any definite response from the audience?
What kind of response?
Is it likely to give the audience a memorable experience?
Was the play worth doing?
If not, why?
What could I have done to heighten the drama on the one hand, and sharpen the comedy on the other?

It's not easy for a director to accept redundancy upon the advent of performances. It can be a depressing, anticlimactic moment, not always compensated by the audience's enjoyment of what was prepared. But is the director really redundant? I believe not. While he has ceased to be an author's interpreter he has become instead a much-needed morale-booster, and should only go backstage with a kind word. This, I think, is extremely important if the director is to foster rapport which should have developed amongst the performers, thus maintaining or improving the standard at which the production started out.

There are compensatory moments of satisfaction when you sit back with your eyes half-closed, watching your production. You may see then that actors weak in rehearsal blossom before an audience and surpass not only the expectations of others, but their own. You also begin to wonder why actors who were strong when rehearsals were young became progressively weaker and lost their glow by the time they reached the audience.

You will, therefore, understand why I ask myself several questions exclusively about the actors:

How were they affected by audience response?
Did they run wild and become undisciplined as they evoked audience laughter?
Or did they maintain their characters?
Were they suitable for their roles?
Did they establish a rapport with the audience?
Did I pace my rehearsals well?
Did I pin too much faith on inexperienced actors?
Did I cast well?

It would, of course, be a mistake for an actor to think that just because he made an audience laugh he was necessarily successful in his role. Before he could ascertain his success, he would have to know *why* the audience laughed. He would have to be sure that the laughter was directed at his stage character and not at himself.

During performances, actors should be alert for laughs and gasps—anything that didn't come in rehearsal because there wasn't an audience. Now is the time to exercise technique and dramatic instinct. It must be remembered that pauses injected into dialogue in rehearsal must not be rushed, because they are there either to manufacture tension or accentuate laugh lines. The quickest way of killing a comedy characterization is by delivering lines through audience laughter. It's always worth waiting just that fraction of a second to say the line as the laughter is halfway down the incline.

The password to success in performance is discipline—discipline to carry out everything as it was rehearsed with other members of the cast.

After the show, performers should clean off their make-up before meeting the audience, thus preventing the meeting of the two worlds of reality and make-believe. (This is against the tradition of good theatre.) Actually, performers should not go to the audience after a show, but wait for the audience to come to them. Nothing embarrasses a member of the public more than finding himself in the position of having to cast a verdict on an actor's bad performance. Even if you've felt you were good, you must stay in your dressing room and wait for reaction or, alternatively, seek it after the show in the Green Room, the theatre's traditional post-performance meeting place.

You can test the success or failure of a play by that moment's pause before the applause begins. If the applause begins moderately the moment the curtain falls, and gradually grows, you may judge that the play is only partially successful. If, on the other hand, there is a moment's stunned silence followed by a simultaneous burst of applause, then you may know that the play has really held the audience. There is no sweeter moment than this to the director and the actors. There may have been times throughout rehearsals when the director had asked himself why he was crazy enough to take on the production, and times when the actors may have been bored or lazy and wondered whether they could skip a rehearsal. But if the play has succeeded, this sweet moment will banish all such thoughts.

Of course there will have been mistakes, but the

night of the show is not the time for comment on these. In his post-performance emotional state it is cruel to criticize an actor, but it can have a very salutary effect if a post-mortem on the play is held at the group's next meeting. In the cold light of day several mistakes will have come to light and if these are discussed they might be avoided next time.

During the weeks of rehearsal, some thought should have been given to how the production was to be sold to the general public. However well-known the play may be, selling it is often one of the most difficult jobs of all. It has never been easy to sell something that cannot be seen or touched, and that's why theatre groups should have a team of people concerned entirely with promotion. There must be a public relations officer whose job it is to contact patrons, newspapers and anyone else whose presence might help publicize the show. Groups will also need a front-of-house manager, or business manager, as he is sometimes called. With the help of ushers, box-office personnel, cloakroom and parking lot attendants, and possibly someone selling coffee in the foyer, the business manager can present the production in its warmest, most friendly form.

Remember, theatre groups realize their income from the front of house and if this is well-organized, the play, be it good, bad or indifferent, will stand a much greater chance of recuperating its expenses or making a profit. Never forget, too, that the front-of-house department is the first and last department seen by the audience as it arrives and leaves the theatre. It is, therefore, destined to make an impression. With this in mind, the front-of-house personnel should be gracious, suitably dressed and helpful. The front-of-house manager should see that members of his team at least know something about the play—its story and its length—and that the box-office personnel maintain an up-to-date seating plan so as to avoid seating confusion just before the rising of the curtain.

When presenting costume plays, actors should always remember to take off items of jewellery. I recall a production of the opera *Turandot* (set in ancient China) given at the O'Keefe Centre in Toronto, in 1965, when despite persistent announcements through the speakers in the dressing rooms, several members of the cast were caught on stage wearing wedding rings and wrist watches. An unforgivable sin!

Finally, actors should always regard their curtain

call as part of the performance, be ready for it and execute it cleanly. Good curtain calls in amateur theatre are becoming increasingly hard to find. If the director decides to give his actors a curtain call (and audiences

have come through the years to expect them), then it must be rehearsed regularly as part of the play.

As their productions improve, many groups like to enter competitive festivals where, apart from vying for an assortment of awards, they are given an impartial assessment of their work by an adjudicator. I am not totally endeared to competitive festivals because I find the distribution of awards ludicrous to say the least. I have seen actors in supporting roles win Best Actor awards, over performers who have worked harder and achieved more in roles that have, in turn, demanded more. Likewise, I've seen the spirits of young actresses snapped by adjudicators who, through an obvious lack of knowledge and understanding of a particular kind of theatre, have been unable to apportion the blame for a production's downfall, and have chosen to expose the

A tatty ending to a tatty show. The costumes and set look ragged. The actors don't know what to do with their hands, and there's no focal point.

performers when, in fact, the director should have been held responsible.

I also find it ludicrous that one person, an adjudicator, having decided who was the best actor, best actress, best stage manager, etc., should then have to decide which was the best play. I once saw a clean, well-paced, well-dressed, well-acted production of Tennessee Williams' *Period of Adjustment* edged out of a regional final of the Dominion Drama Festival of Canada by an untidy, poorly-performed, ill-paced production of *Rashomon* in which, during the famous rape scene, the undisciplined leading man went berserk, sliced the scenery down the middle with his cutlass, lost his trousers and had to play the remainder of the act in his purple jockey shorts. Add to this half a dozen late or non-existent sound cues, the collapse of more scenery and some prompting, and you'll understand why it was a great surprise when *Rashomon* was declared the winner. It was in my opinion a typical example of a group having chosen a play without considering if it had the forces to do it justice.

The adjudicator commended the *Rashomon* cast for its courage, and attacked the cast of *Period of Adjustment* for not trying something more adventurous. So, one of theatre's age-old questions reared up again: "Is it better to be courageous but ambitious in a difficult play, or comfortable and proficient in an old stand-by?" While I think adjudicators must be influenced by ingenuity and courage, they should never overlook the wisdom of the group that is aware of its limitations and chooses the less-pretentious play accordingly. I would still prefer to see that old melodrama *Murder in the Red Barn* done well, with spirit and a sense of style, than *Hamlet* performed atrociously.

You will understand now why many groups are constantly asking, "What *is* a good festival play?" My reply is, "A good play done well," for I believe it's just as possible to win a drama festival with a stylish production of *The Odd Couple* as it is with Arthur Miller's drama, *The Crucible.* There is one proviso, however: Whatever is performed should be performed well.

8) Post-Mortem

What went wrong and why,
comedy versus tragedy, pacing,
farce versus comedy,
relationships, characterizations,
inter-play, playing yourself.

Sometimes, when a man is dying, he directs that his body shall be taken by the doctors and cut up so that medical science may benefit from what is found therein. Performers should act in much the same way. When the play is over they should give themselves—to be cut in pieces—not only for their own cause, but for the cause of Little Theatre.

By way of a post-mortem and to show what kind of goodness may come out of it, I am, in effect, presenting one: an interview with an actress who had a supporting role in the Max Schulman-Robert Paul Smith comedy *The Tender Trap*. Although the audience laughed during this production, the play failed because the laughs were only titters, and there were strong undertones of pathos towards the end of the play which were never brought out. Here is a list of some of its deficiencies:

The only relief from the steady flow of deadpan dialogue, delivered at the same pace and volume throughout, was when an actor created a pause, often in a strategically bad moment, by forgetting a line.

The cuing generally was bad.
More than half the actors were physically unsuitable for their roles—either too young or too old, too fat or too thin.
The combination of English and North American voices was wrong for an American comedy.
The actors moved badly and were given bad, unmotivated moves to negotiate.
The climaxes weren't exploited. They became lost in the steady stream of deadpan dialogue.
Costumes weren't given enough thought. (Even a modern play has to be costumed.)
Make-up was bad.
The play was acted—rather unwisely in this case—on an open, thrust stage, with the audience sitting on three sides.
Besides being hard to look at, the set did nothing for the action.

I'm confining the post-mortem to my conversation with one actress because it is a typical conversation revealing a typical Little Theatre attitude. I'm not even going to explain the play's plot or theme, except to say it's about one man's lust for women, a lust which ends when he's caught in the tender trap. A piquant little blonde hooks him into marriage, ironically, on her own terms.

You'll notice that at one point, the actress decides that she wants someone else's role. This really amounts to an excuse for her inability to deal with her own role satisfactorily. Notice, too, how she accuses the leading man of playing himself, and talks quite inanely of herself in real life and how it relates to her capabilities on stage. More than anything, see how she lavishes blame for the production's downfall on the woman who directed it, and ends the post-mortem with the solid pronouncement that she will have more influence on future productions because she is now publicity chief.

Author: What's the most frustrating thing about the amateur theatre?

Actress: What do I think?

Author: Yes.

Actress: I don't really feel I have any great talent as an actress. I do it simply because I enjoy it. Maybe I'm the kind of person that needs an exciting kind of life and this is an outlet for me. So to me, when I do something, it's terribly important that I be good at it. And this is why I didn't appreciate it when people said, "Oh, you looked gorgeous on stage." and "You looked lovely." because that isn't what I was trying to achieve.

Author: What were you trying to achieve?

Actress: I was trying to be good as an actress. I mean, if I was in a fashion show and they told this to me, then I'd be flattered, but I wasn't flattered in this case because they weren't commenting on my acting.

Author: Do you think you were good as an actress?

Actress: No, I don't think I was. I could have been a lot better.

Author: Who do you blame?

Actress: Well, I feel I blame myself but I feel I know my own limitations and unfortunately I am not that talented and so I need a good director who can pull things out of me. And, unfortunately, as I say, this is what worried me about being in this play with this woman who directed. She wasn't experienced and she couldn't offer me anything. I mean, she didn't tell me a bloody thing.

Author: And what do you think she should have told you?

Actress: Well, you yourself, when you saw the play, said that the comedy wasn't played up enough. I don't know where or how to play for comedy. I don't know this.

Author: Don't you?

Actress: No I don't. Obviously.

Author: Do you know that pacing is the key to good comedy: building up to laugh lines and using pauses to set the laugh lines off?

Actress: I do know that comedy has to be fast. It has to be punched out, and you can't drag a comedy.

Author: Is that all you know about comedy?

Actress: Yes, really.

Author: If I may say so, I can tell you don't know too much about comedy as opposed to other forms of theatre, so let me talk in general terms for the moment. Whereas farce is a type of comedy which exploits the humour of a situation, light comedy gets its humour from its characters. You can see now why it's generally much more important to research characters when you're doing a comedy than it is when you're doing a tragedy.

Actress: Someone else told me this.

Author: Now, to act in a comedy you also require much more technique, comparatively speaking, than you do when you're acting in a tragedy. This is because in comedy you have to strive continuously, sometimes against all odds, to hold the audience's attention, whereas in tragedy, the audience tends to give more of itself rather than to simply sit back and say, "All right, I'm here. Now make me laugh." Let me say it in another way. When it's watching tragedy, the audience's emotional response is more generously given.

Actress: I see what you mean.

Author: Furthermore, comedy is a very nimble form— nimble in situation and nimble in dialogue. If you did a comedy and let it drag, the audience would have little to survive on between one laugh line and the next laugh line, or from one funny incident to the other. Speed is therefore an important element but you also have to consider that too much speed, or the same speed all the way through a play, gets to be monotonous. Pace has to be varied, and you do this, in part, by designing your climaxes and quickening the pace as you build up to lines and climaxes you know are almost certain to draw laughter. And, of course, it goes without saying that, in order to achieve these climaxes, the cuing between actors must be very, very quick so as not to let down the motion that has been set up. So, you see, a comedy is much more than "doing it fast and punching it out," as you put it. Anyway, do you think this play, *The Tender Trap,* was all comedy?

Actress: Well, basically it's a comedy, but you yourself said that you thought that my part had a little more depth than maybe some of the others and also that the philosophy of the writer came out in several of my speeches.

Author: But did the director tell you that although this play was funny, it had some tragic, or pathetic, undertones?

Actress: No, I told you that none of this was ever discussed.

Author: Do you think the play had pathos?

Actress: Well, basically yes, because I was out to get a man and I was the one who was . . . .

Author: Yes, but what about the central character—the man who was out to find himself a woman, and all he had was physical relationships and none of the women ever came back to him?

Actress: Most of them were anxious to get married.

Author: That's right, but did you go into this before the play began rehearsals?

Actress: We hit on it very lightly, but not really to any depth.

Author: Have you ever been in an amateur play where they *have* discussed the characters?

Actress: Yes.

Author: To any depth?

Actress: Oh yes, but, as I say, this is the difference between a professional director like yourself and an amateur director.

Author: What other complaints do you have about the play?

Actress: I don't really know offhand. I'd have to stop and think about it. [Pause] Well, my main complaint was that she [the director] didn't go into characterizations, relationships, interplay, any of this, which I felt she should have done. Somebody was there Saturday night who was in our group when we had the Centre Players and he gave me heck. He says, "You didn't bring in anything that you learnt at your workshop about all this interplay and all this." I says, "I did." I says, "If I didn't have that little bit of training I had in workshop, I would've been really lost because she [the director] didn't go into any of this. I just had to rely on this little bit that I *did* remember."

Author: Do you know how you fitted into this play? Do you know how you should have reacted to all the other characters?

Actress: *How* I should have reacted?

Author: Yes.

Actress: Do you want me to go into my relationships? How I felt?

Author: Yes.

Actress: Well, first of all, I really wasn't in love with Charlie Reader, but I wanted him because I wanted to get married and he was a good prospect. Actually, the way I saw it, I didn't really fall for this Joe but I did ward off his advances because he was a married man. I realized there would be nothing in it for me.

Author: And what else?

Actress: Well, as far as any other relationship, I was on stage a couple of times with a couple of women. Naturally, I didn't like any of the other women because they were a threat to me.

Author: Did you show this?

Actress: Well, I don't know how it came through, but I tried to show a dislike to Julie Gillis. That's why I made fun of her—you know that little scene we had where we were imitating her?

Author: Yes.

Actress: I don't know if it came through, but I certainly wasn't . . . .

Author: What about the movement? Did the director discuss or tell you that she was going to help you show this dislike by moving you in a certain way?

Actress: Not at all .

Author: ... by keeping you apart, or ....

Actress: No.

Author: If you don't like a person, you don't go and sit next to her on the chesterfield, do you?

Actress: Not necessarily.

Author: No, but initially you would try to keep away from her, wouldn't you?

Actress: I would think so.

Author: Did you go into this?

Actress: No, not at all.

Author: Did the director discuss with the leading man, around whom the whole play spindles, that when a man has, say, six or seven girl friends, as this man did, he would possibly have each one, perhaps, for a slightly different reason. Basically, he would probably want sex from them. One would suppose from the script that he was getting it. But he would have, nevertheless, a slightly different relationship with each, wouldn't he? Some relationships would be purely physical, some might be spiritual and physical, and there would be other things, too, wouldn't there?

Actress: Well, I would think so because even in the lines it says that Sylvia was a different kind of girl. She didn't ....

Author: But you agree with me?

Actress: Yes—and he wouldn't have got anywhere with her. He was telling this to his friends.

Author: All right, but did the director discuss with the leading man and this actress that this aspect should have come through in the play?

Actress: No. This is why I wanted the part of the girl in the beginning—this Poppy—because I felt that his relationship with her was purely sexual.

Author: Do you think you would have been right for this part of Poppy?

Actress: I don't know. I think I could have done it. It was a character role. I thought I could have done more with it, whereas mine was pretty straightforward.

Author: Do you think you would have been the right type?

Actress: Why not? You don't think so?

Author: No, because she was a very outward-going kind of person, a character who tended to be very much larger than life. I notice your director played her as a blousy girl and you're very much a sophisticated woman, aren't you?

Actress: Yes, but I think they were all sophisticated to a point, except maybe Julie, because they were all women of about thirty and they'd been around New York and they all had good positions. None of them were really stupid. He [the playwright] said that Poppy was an editor at Doubleday's.

Author: All right, looking at your production, do you think that Poppy looked like a book editor or spoke like one?

Actress: No.

Author: Why?

Actress: Well, she was miscast.

Author: What about the other characters? Do you think that some of those were miscast?

Actress: I think they were, too.

Author: Who do you blame?

Actress: That was the casting.

Author: But who do you blame?

Actress: The only thing is, we haven't got the right characters to work with in the group. Don't you have to develop them the way you want?

Author: Don't you think you should go outside a group for people?

Actress: Oh, yes.

Author: Did the director make any effort to do this?

Actress: Only for the male lead because she felt that was important. He carried the play.

Author: All right. That's very good to assume that the main character carries the play. But, don't you think . . . .

Actress: Don't you think he carried the play?

Author: Let me answer your question. Don't you think that the women were also very important since the play depended on a series of relationships amongst people?

Actress: Well, I think this helps mould the whole thing together.

Author: Mould, be damned! It does much more than that. It's the difference between the whole thing being believable or being unbelievable.

Actress: What did you think about the male lead? Did you think he . . . . I mean, considering it was his first play . . . .

Author: I think he did extremely well, but you see he

had within him intelligence and a natural sense of theatre, and his natural sense of theatre told him not only *how* to react and move, but *why* he was doing this. An awful lot of the other characters were moving because they felt they wanted to show the audience the other side of their faces. And the director, I must add here, gave far too much movement and most of it was unmotivated. The production was very, very restless.

Actress: Do you feel though . . . this is something that I've wondered . . . . Now, she wanted this person, this male lead, very typecast. And this guy, I feel, and I really got to know him since I was in the play with him—when he was in my Mutual Funds office I never said a couple of words to him—I believe he is acting this every day of his life. I don't think he's this great big playboy that he tries to let on.

Author: What are you trying to say—that he was playing himself?

Actress: That he was playing himself. This is the story of his life. He's acting this every day of his life. Now, I wonder if he was thrown into another kind of role whether he'd be lost. Say, if he played something completely remote, say . . . .

Author: He may well be, but there are many actors who only ever play themselves. I would say that most actors only really ever play themselves, even many of the so-called great film stars— John Wayne, for instance.

Actress: But you said he had a feeling for the theatre because he moved well.

Author: Yes, I said he had a natural sense of theatre, sure—not only because he moved well, but for other reasons. But this doesn't mean that he's going to be versatile in the roles he can play, does it?

Actress: This is why I wonder if he'd ever be able to play another kind of role.

Author: Well, why not? I'm not going to write him off, but I'm saying that in this part he was absolutely right.

Actress: Oh, I agree.

Author: And I'm prepared to agree also that he probably only ever played himself. But there's no sin in playing yourself. John Wayne has done it for years. Cary Grant has done it for years. I think Sidney Poitier plays himself a great deal. I think if you look at the world's most proficient actors . . . .

Actress: But don't you think you're limited as an actor if you can't be versatile?

Author: Yes, certainly, but when you're making millions from one movie, who cares whether you're versatile or not? If you look at the world's great actors, people who can play virtually anything or many different kinds of roles, there are relatively few. I repeat— relatively few.

Actress: That can play any kind of a role?

Author: . . . like Sir Alec Guinness, Sir Laurence Olivier and Rod Steiger, to name just three. They've shown us they can master a wide assortment of parts.

Actress: Yes, I see what you mean now.

Author: Anyway, let's get back to *The Tender Trap*. If you could do this part again, what would you do differently?

Actress: Well, basically I think I'd have to play the comedy up. I mean, I know that was one of the faults. What would you suggest?

Author: I would suggest that you look more deeply into the play as to not only how *you* fit into it but how *other people* fit into it. If I were to ask you what was ironic about the play, could you tell me?

Actress: I don't think so.

Author: Do you know what irony is? [Pause] You do?

Actress: Yes.

Author: Would you know if there were any other elements of good literature in this play? Do you think the dialogue was good? Do you think the plot was good?

Actress: Do you think the dialogue was good?

Author: Yes, I think it was very good. But I think that for a comedy it was underplayed. It wasn't nearly funny enough. This is the kind of play that depends so heavily on its humour. Some plays, of course, are written in such a way that the humour is secondary to the pathos, but this was not one of those plays. And so, essentially, the play should have been funny. It wasn't funny. In that respect it failed—

miserably. So, bearing these things in mind, what would you do if you had the role again—the same role with the same director?

Actress: Well, just the things that we've discussed. We'd have to go into them more. But then, as I say, if I had to do it with the same director again, I'd still be up the same paddle without a creek. I mean, I'd still be up the creek without a paddle, because I still wouldn't know where to play up the humour, because I don't know. I need a director to tell me.

Author: Have you got a sense of humour?

Actress: Yes, I think I do—have a sense of humour.

Author: Do you mean to say that you read lines in this very funny script and you couldn't see the humour in them?

Actress: But then I was playing them wrong, you see, because this is what I do in real life—I laugh at my own jokes. I was doing that, but I wasn't getting the laughs.

Author: You realize, too, that some people are funny because they're deadpan, and sometimes if we laugh at our own jokes on stage we destroy or detract from the humour.

Actress: Yes. I was doing that. I was laughing at my own jokes, like the one you told me about the line, "Well, it keeps me off the streets." And you told me to do it deadpan and to drink the coffee afterwards.

Author: Yes. I wanted you to punctuate the line with the coffee cup so you wouldn't look as though you were sitting there with nothing to do—just waiting for the audience to laugh.

Actress: Well, I did it that way Friday night and I got a big laugh. I did it how you told me. I don't know whether you remember it.

Author: And what do you think was the reason for your getting the laugh?

Actress: Well, I did it deadpan—the way you told me to. But up till then I was making a joke out of it. I'd say, "Well, it keeps me off the streets," and I'd give a big laugh. That was the way I was doing it.

Author: Yes, but you see, this brings me to another point about playing comedy. One of the most common faults of amateurs is that they are not consistent. They tend to step from the comic into the farcical. By laughing at your own joke when you said your line, you stepped out of the skin of the comedy character you'd created, and maintained for much of the play, and became unbelievable; unbelievable just for that moment. The audience felt this, although they probably didn't know quite what was wrong—audiences seldom do—and the line didn't get the laughter that was due to it. The audience's attention had been directed elsewhere. However, when you delivered the line nonchalantly, deadpan and in character, it was funny.

Actress: This is me in real life. I laugh at my own jokes.

Author: Did the director try to stop this? Did she see you were stepping out of character by laughing at your own joke in the play, do you think?

Actress: No, she didn't.

Author: What was the reaction of other people in the cast? Did they think the play was successful?

Actress: Well, as I say, with their limited experience, they probably all did.

Author: Do you realize that most amateur plays fail even though audiences think they're funny. They fail in so far as they don't put across what the author is trying to say . . . .

Actress: Because, maybe, they don't have the understanding? Is this it?

Author: . . . and the depth, too, don't you think?

Actress: Yes.

Author: Basically, I think, your play lacked depth, and I think the director was to blame. People walking off the set in a play without going through a recognized entrance, in fact, walk out of the play for that moment. In a drawing-room comedy, entrances are there for people to enter through and go out of. If they come in or go out through any other doorway that is not recognized by the audience to be legitimate, then they walk out of the play. The believability of the environment just collapses.

Actress: I think the way they were trying to do it . . . . I don't know, I didn't go into it too much with them . . . . I think they didn't have much of a set and it was supposed to be more suggestive . . . .

Author: All right, but they should have made where

they went valid exits by lighting them. I think they should bear this in mind if they want to do this kind of play again. In other words, this was the kind of play that needed a proscenium arch. You've probably heard me say it many times before: history has proved a proscenium arch to be necessary. Some plays need a proscenium arch because the proscenium arch hides many sins. Other plays can be done very effectively without it, but not American drawing-room comedies or any other drawing-room comedy. The thrust stage or theatre-in-the-round gives this kind of play an extra visual dimension that it doesn't know what to do with. Right?

Actress: Yes.

Author: You agree, then?

Actress: Oh, they were told not to do it this way. One of your colleagues, that English professor, came and told them that this was not the way the play should be done.

Author: Then why did they go ahead and do it?

Actress: They'd made up their minds and that was *it*.

Author: Are they persistently guilty of not taking the advice of a professional?

Actress: They had made up their minds and you can't tell these people anything.

Author: Does that worry you about future productions?

Actress: Well, I feel now I have a little more to say there than I did before in the group. You know the way I look at it, this isn't a great attitude to take, but you see I'm on the executive now. I'm in charge of publicity.

9 Make-up

Its art, how it's affected by lighting, "straight" make-up, character make-up, observing prototypes, the ideal make-up kit, combinations for the straight make-up, how to "grow" old, beards, moustaches, other facial disfigurations.

In the histories covering thirty centuries of theatre we find negligible record of the art of make-up. From the earliest days, right on through the Renaissance era and for some time afterwards, the actor made his stage appearance behind a mask. Not until the advent of Shakespeare do we have the first authentic records of make-up being used by the more famous actors. The greatest advance in the art of make-up, however, occurred in the first quarter of this century, and was due chiefly to the remarkable development of the motion picture industry. The exacting demands of the camera called for make-up to show its highest skill and thus it has become one of the important elements in dramatic production. Certainly it is one of the most fascinating attributes of an actor's craft, and yet, often one of the most neglected. Nearly all amateur actors like to be made-up but, when it is suggested that they learn to do it for themselves, they shrink back with fright.

Make-up is not as difficult as many people imagine. Primarily, it's a matter of common sense, coupled with observation and agility that comes with practice. After all, many young women carry out successful transformations of their faces every day, and stage make-up, though it differs from daily make-up, is not much more difficult to apply. There are, however, basic rules to be learned and learned thoroughly before a good stage make-up can be successfully produced at the first attempt. There are numerous books on the subject from which a great deal may be learned, but too slavish an adherance to illustrations and insufficient use of the imagination sometimes produce startling and unhappy results. It is understandable, therefore, why many amateur actors go on stage to play fairies and butlers, looking like Red Indians, and how the most masculine of men, built like bulls, have been seen cavorting around the stage with cupid lips of cherry red!

It must be remembered at all time that make-up is not a rigid science. It's an art which offers a wide latitude for individual methods and personal technique. While it is very important to know how to apply it correctly, it is equally valuable to know which colours to use. The portrait painter uses colour to create the illusion of depth upon the flat surface of his canvas; the performer uses colour to preserve depth and form against the absorption of intense stage lighting. To put it another way, make-up puts back into the face what lights take out. The lighting system of the stage is such

In the skilled hands of make-up artist Hilda Healy, actor David Mallis slips away and emerges instead as Fagan in Lionel Bart's *Oliver!* (staged by the Hamilton Players' Guild and directed by Maurice Evans). *The Hamilton Spectator*

that it absorbs all the natural colour of the complexion and thus considerably changes the appearance of the performer. Place a beautiful woman without make-up in the brilliance of modern stage lighting and her face will be colourless, her eyes will lose their sparkle, and she will not be the same beautiful woman. Make-up is therefore necessary to restore the natural tone of her complexion which is lost under stage lighting, and to define the features so that she will appear to best advantage from all parts of the theatre. Make-up covers up facial blemishes, too, and helps give the appearance called for by the play. With make-up on, the performer also gets more "feel" of the part being played.

Light can play strange pranks with an actor's face. It can make it appear flat if the *wrong colours* have been used. Every lighting condition has a definite effect on the colour of make-up and this should explain why it's vital for make-up to be worn at both dress rehearsals. When intensive light is used to flood the stage—particularly with amber or straw gelatines—the colour of the make-up must be able to withstand the colour absorption properties of the illumination. This often makes necessary a florid make-up, to preserve a natural appearance. Red and blue lights will always absorb their own colours in the make-up. No amount of dry rouge on the cheeks is ever visible when the stage is flooded with solid red lights, which are used only for special effects. Evening and moonlight scenes are effected by blue gelatines. When blue lights are used, the performer should always subdue any red cheek colour with face powder, because under blue light red turns dark.

The practice of replacing colour and emphasizing features is called "straight" make-up. The depth of colour and the amount of light and shade applied is the important factor here, *not* the amount of make-up put on. It is always better to err in the direction of being *under*-made-up than being over-made-up because it is easier to add to what is already on the face than to have to take off make-up. Furthermore, if make-up is obvious to the audience, then it has been badly applied. Another important aspect to consider is that, generally speaking, the large theatre with powerful stage lighting calls for stronger make-up. In smaller theatres, where the audience is closer to the playing area, the performers need wear hardly any make-up at all. Indeed, I have directed plays in which the actors have played *without* make-up. But whatever make-up is necessary must be applied and examined under conditions similar to those on stage. It's no use making-up by the light of a sixty-watt lamp hung high in the dressing room—because this will not give a fair indication of what the finished effect will look like under the powerful lights of the stage. Just as the painter seeks light to define his colours, the actor applying his own make-up must seek light to help him seek the characteristics in his face. (Straight make-up is simply a process of amplifying existing features and seeing true colour.)

There is another use for make-up: to change the features so they correspond with the character in the script, for however convincing an actor might be, the audience will not accept his portrayal unless the physical characteristics are well enough defined. If, for instance, he is playing an old man, the audience expects to see just that—an old man with old hands, an old man's face and an old man's walk. In much the same way, the audience will not accept that the actor is dying of starvation if he still wears the rounded bloom of youth.

If we are to be proficient in the art of "character" make-up we must develop our powers of observation so much to the full that we eventually have an obsession for studying the faces of men and women, young and old, whom we meet every day of our lives. More than this, we must spot what makes them unique. When we look around us we see that the change from youth to maturity manifests itself in similar ways. In the aged man or woman the facial muscles sag and lose their elasticity, fat disappears, the skin wrinkles and becomes loose on the cheek and neck, teeth go, the line of the mouth changes, the lips are thinner, the complexion is sallow or pale, the hair becomes sparse and the formation of the head is more apparent. All these physical changes must be understood before we can make the transformation from youth to maturity. But the more subtle differences among older people will be in their natures, their temperaments, their personalities. Much stress, however, must be laid on the face because it furnishes an index of a person's character and his experiences, and is significant, therefore, in dramatic characterization.

To the serious make-up student, the study of faces will never cease to be of interest, and the success of what he is able to produce will always be relative to the amount of intelligence with which he "sees" the expression which characterizes the personality to be

Chinese type make-up

Men	Women
Grease paint #12	5
Face powder #12	12
Moist rouge #4	3
Lining colour #2	22
Eyebrow pencil: black	black

Beards and moustaches indicate distinctly the type and station of the Oriental character. Varying shades, from black to white, denote age. A long, drooping moustache bespeaks the scholar, while a short one denotes a rude and unrefined character. Art work: Max Factor.

The pirate
has an outdoor complexion and is usually swarthy. The following make-up material is suggested:

Grease paint #7
Face powder #16
Moist rouge #4
Lining colours #21/12
Eyebrow pencil
Collodion, for scars
Nose putty
Crepe hair

Note: the missing tooth gives a realistic touch.
Art work: Max Factor

portrayed. Books can only show the way. Success in the art of make-up comes by an instinctive feeling of the part to be played, by studious observation of prototypes, and by acquiring a deftness in handling the materials. In the hands of one actor the finest make-up materials may result in a masterful impersonation; in the hands of another actor, these same materials may reveal only ignorance or stupidity. This recalls to mind the great painter who when asked, "With what do you mix your paints?" answered, "With brains, Sir."

Many of the more affluent Little Theatre groups go to the expense of hiring a make-up artist to work on the entire cast. Sometimes, though not always, the make-up artist attends the dress rehearsals as well as the performance, but rarely does he see the play in rehearsal. The outcome is that he has a preconceived idea of what the character should look like, and makes him up accordingly, without having read the play and spoken to the director about how that character is being portrayed. The actor relaxes in his chair with his eyes closed (for being made-up has a soothing effect) and the make-up artist begins his work. A few minutes later, when the actor opens his eyes and looks in the mirror, he sees he has slipped away and another person has emerged in his place. But this other person who stares back does not coincide with the character the actor is feeling inside. Interior and exterior must match, and only the actor can unite the two. Perhaps more performers should be taught to apply their own make-up.

By all means engage a make-up expert, but make sure he attends rehearsals, and let him teach the performers something of his art.

Theatre make-up comes in several forms. It is available in grease paint sticks and tubes, and also as a pre-mixed, greaseless substance called pancake which can be applied with a wet sponge. Although it tends to subside against the profuse perspiring to which an actor is subjected under harsh stage lights, many people still prefer to use grease paint. This is partly because they are afraid to depart from tradition and partly because grease paint has the reputation—quite falsely I think—of being more versatile. However, it has now become more general among make-up artists to use make-up in its greaseless form because it can be spread quicker and more evenly, is cleaner to work with, and counteracts perspiration because it dries the skin and fills the pores.

It is not the purpose of this book to state a

preference because each has its advantages and disadvantages, but from now on I will refer to either "make-up" or "grease paint" as being the same thing. Both the pancake and the grease sticks and tubes can be bought in corresponding numbers, and the suggestions I put forth are therefore adjustable.

While I consider it imperative for every actor to have his own make-up—especially if he is to be able to practise—some groups prefer to have a communal kit. The following suggested kit contains virtually everything that would be needed, even for the most ambitious of productions, and can be bought for less than $100.

The skipper
is normally portrayed as a man of fifty or older. He does not normally wear a moustache, and his beard is trimmed to make his full chin visible. He has heavy, low eyebrows, to match his beard and wig. The rest of his expression is created by the use of lining colours. Deep furrows are effected by the careful application of shadows and highlights.

Suggested make-up:
Ground colour:
Grease paint #7A
Face powder #9
Dark brown
dermatograph pencil
Lining colour for
wrinkles and
shadows: #22
Lining colour for
highlights: #12
Lip rouge:
Dark red #4
Medium brown and grey
crepe hair, for beard and
eyebrows
Art work: Max Factor

Grease Paint
1½ - Light Pink
2A - Juvenile
4½ - Cream
5½ - Orange
6   - Sallow
7A - Dark Sunburn
8A - East Indian
10 - Indian
12 - Mikado

Pancake
2A - Juvenile
7A - Dark Sunburn

Face Powder
2   - Light Pink
7R - Rachelle
9   - Sunburn
16 - Spanish

Lining Colours
1   - Black
2   - Dark Brown
6   - Blue-grey
22 - Medium Brown

Dermatograph Pencils
Brown, Black

Moist Rouge
Light, Medium, Dark

96

The tramp
Suggested make-up:

Use 6A grease paint for the ground colour of the complexion. Blend aged lines and wrinkles around the eyes. With a brown pencil, smudge the lines into the ground colour. Curve the corners of the mouth upwards, using lip rouge No. 3. If it is necessary to change the contour of the face, such as the nose, chin or cheek bones, use nose putty. To block out teeth, use black tooth enamel. This is very effective for those whose teeth are very prominent. The make-up should then be completely powdered, with No. 5 face powder, and the surplus should be carefully brushed off before any hair is applied. Note the character of the false moustache and the beard. Art work: Max Factor

Under Rouge
Rose, Brunette, Carmine

Dry Rouge
Raspberry
Theatrical No. 18
Blondeen
Technicolour

Miscellaneous
Clown White
Black Tooth Enamel
Nose Putty
Cosmetic Black
Spirit Gum
Powder Puffs (2)
Cleansing Cream
Liquid Body Make-up
Paper Liners (2 packages)
Eyelash Make-Up—Black
Masque, for Greying Hair—White
Eyebrow Brush
Camel's Hair Brushes (2)
Brillox—Brilliantine
Sponge

Crepe Hair
(For Beards, Moustaches, etc.)
Black
Dark Brown
Medium Brown
Light Brown
Iron Grey
Light Grey

A smaller kit of basic grease paint sticks for the individual can be compiled for about fifteen dollars. I suggest:

Grease Paint
Standard-size stick
Form C
No. 1 - Whitish
No. 2 - Pinkish
No. 3 - Rose
No. 4 - Ivory-Yellow
No. 9 - Brown-Red

Carmine
Form H
No. 1, No. 2, No. 3

Lining Colours
Form E
No. 22 - White
No. 25 - Lake
No. 28 - Brown
No. 42 - Black
No. 326 - Dark Blue

Miscellaneous
Tin of Dark Blending Powder
Tin of Light Blending Powder
Eyebrow Pencils, one black, one brown
Bottle of Liquid Cream Mascara (black)
One foot of Crepe Hair
Bottle of Spirit Gum

Additionally, it's necessary to have:

A mirror in which the whole face can be seen at the
same time
Paint brushes for lines and finish
Toothpicks, for adding the lines
Facial tissues
Old towels
Hairbrush and comb
Newspapers on which to lay out the make-up

From the larger kit, the combination of grease
paint sticks No. 5 and No. 9, widely used in traditional
straight make-up, is not given. This is because, as I have
already said, make-up is not a rigid science. Other, more
modern combinations for the straight make-up were
compiled when it was found that the use of grease paint
sticks No. 5 and No. 9 did not make sufficient allow-
ances for varying skin types and hair colourings among
actors. (See the *Suggested Guide for Straight Make-Up,*
where light combinations are offered.)

Here's a suggested step-by-step way of making up
young persons as older characters:

1. Apply ground colour grease No. 5½ to face and neck. It
   must be spread smoothly and evenly.
2. Mark wrinkles in the forehead between the eyes, under

the eyes, at the outer corners of the eyes, and from the nostrils to the outer corners of the mouth, with a dark brown pencil. All wrinkles should be marked *only* where wrinkles form naturally. The edges of these lines should be blended softly into the foundation, and each wrinkle must be highlighted with a contrasting colour, using lining colour No. 12 (white). The highlight is applied with a paper stump or a tinting brush, adjacent to the wrinkle. The edges of the highlight and wrinkle should be blended carefully together and into the foundation.

3. In making hollow cheeks, temples or sunken eyes, blend a darker colour than the foundation into the cheeks, under the eyes, or wherever the sunken effect is desired, using a No. 2 (dark brown) lining colour. To accentuate the cheekbones, highlight them with No. 12 lining colour. The edges of the lids next to the lashes may be slightly coloured with red. This will dull the expression of the eyes. A puffy effect is created, also with No. 2 (dark brown), by blending it immediately under the lower lid. This is highlighted with white, and the lower edge of this highlight is then shadowed. This effect must be worked out carefully according to the shape and size of the eyes. Proceed in the same manner on the upper lid.

4. A decided lip line is barely apparent in old people, and a thinner one must be created. First, block out the natural lips with foundation make-up. Replace thin lips with No. 3 lip colour, either on its own or mixed with a No. 6 grey lining colour. A shrivelled appearance can be given to the mouth by drawing short vertical lines on the upper and lower lips with a dark brown dermatograph pencil. For decrepit and derelict types, a realistic touch is effected by blocking out one or two teeth with black tooth enamel. Drooping the corners of the mouth will give the character a careworn or sad expression.

5. After the character lines and shadows have been satis-factorily applied, pat face powder over the entire make-up. Then remove surplus powder with a soft face brush. A dry rouge (colour naturelle) is used to accentuate the hollow areas of the cheeks and temples, which have been shadowed.

6. No character make-up is complete without the proper arrangement of the hair and treatment of the eyebrows. They must be in keeping with the type represented. A wig sometimes becomes an important accessory to aid the evolution from youth to maturity. It's always best, however, to try to do something with the actor's own

hair. Good wigs are expensive to rent and are not always satisfactory. They move about and are uncomfortably hot. Hair can be whitened or greyed to varying degrees with powder, white grease paint, or hair spray. Although it catches the light and, at times, tends to look unreal, hair spray has become popular with amateur groups. Remember: eyebrows are generally the same colour as the hair. Very rarely will you find an even greyness in the hair of a middle-aged person. Normally, traces of the original colour show through.

7. (The application of beards and moustaches will be discussed shortly.)

Extreme old age calls for practically the same treatment except that the wrinkles are more numerous, the hollow and sunken parts more noticeable, and the lip line hardly visible. If the rule of accentuating only that which is already in the face is strictly adhered to, a young actor made up to play an old-age part should resemble what he will appear late in his life. It is also worth repeating here that make-up has two tasks. First, the colour must accentuate the general form and the shape of the face. Second, the eyebrow pencil, lip rouge, eye shadow and dry rouge must define the features. It is an erroneous notion that "any old way" will do when making-up. The art is full of details, and to be slipshod about any one of them may affect the success of a performance. A careless smudge of grease paint might give an actor an extra wrinkle, dimple, shadow or other slight facial distortion he could well do without. Good make-up creates an illusion, but there is no illusion about poor make-up. No matter how far back on the stage you are, or how unimportant your part, it is not good stagecraft to face an audience with poor make-up. The work calls for studied detail, and on the stage, especially, there's nothing trivial about detail.

Applying Beards and Moustaches

The best beards are made of real hair which is knotted on net. These are stuck on the face with spirit gum. Real beards are, however, expensive. Quite satisfactory beards can be made of crepe hair which is plaited on a string. Unless an unkempt beard is required, crepe hair must be relieved of some of its crinkle before use. Don't take out all the crinkle because the crepe hair will then become limp and unmanageable. Enough crinkle is removed by passing the crepe hair two or three times through the steam of a boiling kettle. Crepe hair lacks the lustre of real hair, and it is advisable to choose a shade of beard that is slightly lighter than the hair of the head. Experience will tell how much crepe hair to use; most people tend to use too much. The really important thing is that the beard should jut out and not straggle feebly down the chin.

After the crimp has been taken out, cut three pieces from the plait, each about five to six inches long. Tease out each piece until the knots are removed and it is about three inches wide. Gently pull one of the pieces in half so that there are four pieces in all: two of them three inches wide and five to six inches long, and two one-and-a-half inches wide and five inches long. The larger pieces form the centre of the beard on top and under the chin and the two narrower pieces form the sides. Before beginning the next operation, it is advisable to have a damp towel ready, otherwise there might be more hair on the ends of the fingers than on the chin. Paint the underside of the chin with spirit gum. Be sure to take this well back, nearly as far as the Adam's apple. Then apply the crepe hair so that the ends jut out three inches beyond the chin. Press the crepe hair firmly into place with the damp towel. Now the upper part of the chin has to be painted with spirit gum, following the growth line of the natural beard, higher in the centre of the chin and curving down to the corners of the mouth. The crepe hair must be placed into position and pressed down with the towel, so it will fall the way it would naturally grow. Paint the jawbone on either side and apply the two narrow pieces so that they jut forward and mingle with the hair on top and under the chin. Actually, each layer of hair should overlap the other, just as shingles are applied to the roof of a house. Allow the spirit gum to dry for a few minutes, then gently squeeze the pieces together so that the separate ones cannot be seen. With a pair of sharp scissors, barber the beard to the required shape.

If a moustache is also required, take about an inch of crepe hair, from which the crinkle has been partially removed, and paint the upper lip with spirit gum. Then cut the piece of crepe hair across the middle, and apply one piece and then the other on either side of the hollow in the centre of the upper lip, being careful to leave a gap between the hair. Press with a damp towel and, when dry, trim to the natural growth. Remember, in an actual moustache the natural growth of hair follows the curve of the lip line. Beards and moustaches are easily removed with surgical spirit or rubbing alcohol, which quickly dissolves the spirit gum.

Unshaven Effect

There are two methods of achieving the unshaven effect: by using grey-blue or warm brown lining colour, either of which when stippled (not smeared as is commonly the case) will look authentic; by using small pieces of crepe hair. Distribute the hair, cut into pieces about an eighth of an inch long, over the surface of a smooth towel and transfer them to the face, covered sparingly with spirit gum. If the hair is distributed equally, the effect will look natural.

General Facial Disfigurations

Nose putty, a soft, plastic material sometimes referred to as nose paste, has a million uses for effecting complete disguises. Applied to such places as the nose, chin and cheekbones, it can alter the contours of the face to represent innumerable comic, grotesque and racial types. Providing they are not too heavy, even the eyebrows may be concealed with nose putty.

Nose putty must, of course, be applied to the face before the rest of the make-up. Kneading it between the fingers will make it soft and extra pliability will be gained by mixing it with grease paint. A little spirit gum should also be worked into the mixture to counteract perspiration and ensure adhesiveness.

Scars

When it becomes necessary to make a scar we should understand its construction and the art of obtaining a realistic effect. There are many methods but I will only describe the more simple ones known to the theatrical profession.

The average scar appears as a welt—and not as an indentation. It's caused by a blow and is somewhat different from that caused by a knife wound. This type of scar can be created by nose putty, built up in the centre and smoothed off at the edges into the foundation make-up. The raised surface may be coloured with a grey-blue lining colour No. 6, accentuating the bruised part of the welted scar. The line of a scar should be irregular and never straight.

Nose putty may also be used for creating indentions. Spread it well over the spot where the scar is wanted, raising up the centre and smoothing the edges into the complexion. Make a crease in the centre, line it with warm brown (No. 22 lining colour), highlight it with a No. 12 white and blend the edges well together. Another method of making indentions is with non-flexible collodion, which is painted on and treated in the same way as the nose putty. Three or four applications of collodion are usually sufficient.

Old surface scars are discolourations, and may be of any conceivable size or colour. The dark parts of scars require a lowlight—a No. 22 lining colour, warm brown. Highlight the edges with a contrasting colour, a No. 12 white. The illusion is completed when the edges are carefully blended. Some scars can be made to appear very natural by touching up here and there with a little purple, No. 8.

Grade seven and eight students from Toronto schools in a production of Shakespeare's "Macbeth" directed by Maurice E. Evans. Notice the effective use of tooth enamel.

Suggested guide for straight make-up

The following chart will give you approximately the correct shades for various types. The colour scheme of "in-between" types may vary, i.e., a blond type may have hazel or grey eyes, a brunette may have blue or grey eyes, but ordinarily, the colour of both the hair and eyes distinguishes the blonde from the brunette, as follows:

Blondes: blonde hair, blue eyes, fair skin.
Brunettes: dark hair, dark eyes, medium skin.

	Girl Juvenile		*Men Juvenile*	
	Blonde	Brunette	Blonde	Brunette
Grease Paint	4A	4½-2A	6A	7A
Face Powder	7R	8	9	9
Lining Colour	16	22	2	2
Moist Rouge	1	1	3	3
Under-Rouge	2	3-2	3	4
Derma. Pencil	Brown	Black	Brown	Black
Dry Rouge	Blondeen	18	Raspberry	Raspberry
Masque	Dk. Brown	Black	None	None
Liq. Body Make-up	1½	4A	None	None

	Children		*Elderly types*	
	Female	Male	Women	Men
Grease Paint	2	2A	4½	5½
Face Powder	6	7R	7R	9
Lining Colour	16	6	6	3
Moist Rouge	1	2	3-2	3
Under-Rouge	2	3	3	2
Derma. Pencil	Brown	Brown	Brown	Black
Dry Rouge	Blondeen	Raspberry	Raspberry	Natural
Masque	Brown	None	Brown	None
Liq. Body Make-up	1A	4	None	None

Pan-cake make-up in corresponding or similar colours may be used in place of grease paint.

Suggested make-up for middle and old age types

Female types

	Middle Age	Old Age
Grease Paint	4½	5
Face Powder	7R	8
Moist Rouge	3	3
Lining Colours		
For Highlights	12	12
For Eyeshadow	6	2
For Sunken Effects	2	2
Dry Rouge	Natural	12
Derma. Pencil	Dark Brown	Dark Brown
Liquid Make-up	5	5

Male types

	Middle Age	Old Age
Grease Paint	5½	5½ or 6
Face Powder	8	17
Moist Rouge	3	3
Lining Colours		
For Eyeshadow	2	2
For Highlights	12	12
For Sunken Effects	2	2
Dry Rouge	Natural	None
Derma. Pencil	Dark Brown	Dark Brown

Reading List
Bramford, T. W. *Practical Make-up for the Stage* (Pitman).
Corson, Richard, *Stage Make-up* (Appleton-Century-Crofts).
Melvill, Harald, *Magic of Make-up* (Rockliff).

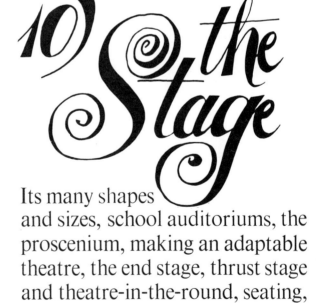

10) the Stage

Its many shapes and sizes, school auditoriums, the proscenium, making an adaptable theatre, the end stage, thrust stage and theatre-in-the-round, seating, sightlines, auditorium entrances.

The Little Theatre group's most formidable hindrance in its struggle for survival is quite often the place in which it presents its plays. The usual provision is a local hall, a school auditorium or even a gymnasium where the audience has to crane to watch the action from the first few rows, because the stage is too high. In many cases, especially in some of the older halls and auditoriums, there's an abundance of distracting decorative detail and hollow acoustics. Stage lighting, such as it is, is confined behind the proscenium arch because provision was never made for front-of-house spots, and the chances of erecting them on a temporary basis are negligible because there is often nothing on which to hang them.

Apart from being dramatically unfunctional, facilities in some of the most modern high schools are obsolete before they are even completed. Stages are not always designed for flexibility, and auditoriums are known to bear some of the old traits—too many glossy surfaces, ornamentation stuck above the proscenium arch, carelessly designed lighting, and a general sterility which does not help the actor reach the people. Drama should be a passionate affair between the performer and his audience. Alas, it is difficult to be passionate in a school auditorium. The most common excuse is, "Well, we have to use it for many things such as assemblies and lectures and we only put on a play twice a year." That does not excuse the deficiencies. Better design would not necessarily cost more. I know one school auditorium built within the past five years that has a glorious glossy stage and an apron more than twice the size of the playing area behind the curtain. These are the least of its problems, however. The wings are only four feet wide on either side and, rather incredulously, the designers forgot to allow for doors leading from the school corridors to the backstage area! The only route backstage, therefore, is across the gloriously glossy apron and between the curtains.

I've directed plays in high school auditoriums where the local board of education has stipulated that a student, although he may know nothing about lighting, let alone the play being performed, must run the lighting panel. A greater sin in many of the new school auditoriums, however, is to drive a nail into the stage to secure part of the scenery. Why spend so much money laying a highly-polished cedar floor, when the first thing that must be done at dress rehearsal is cover it up so it doesn't catch the light? The extra cost of giving the stage

A school gymnasium was converted into a thrust stage with portable rostrums for Jean Anouilh's *Ondine* (directed at a Roman Catholic high school by the Reverend John Hulley).

a lavish gloss would be better spent on additional lighting or an extra door.

Why suffer the inconveniences? Why permit bureaucracy to regulate the quality and price of amateur theatre? I'd much rather see Little Theatre groups in warehouses where they could be left to their own devices. While warehouses have their own problems, they're considerably cheaper to rent and much more prone to intimacy—a quality on which the future of "live" theatre virtually now depends.

Little Theatre groups are not always so naïve as to be unaware of the disadvantages of playing in public places. Conversely, they do not show the kind of ingenuity that will one day lift them out of such dependence. A theatre of their own is a dream. It remains a dream for a long time, yet just around the corner is an empty warehouse. No one sees it as a possibility because it does not coincide with the general conception of how a theatre should really look.

For the past three hundred years, a single form of theatre has reigned across the world—theatre played on a flat stage against an end wall and framed within an arch we call the proscenium. There were, of course, other

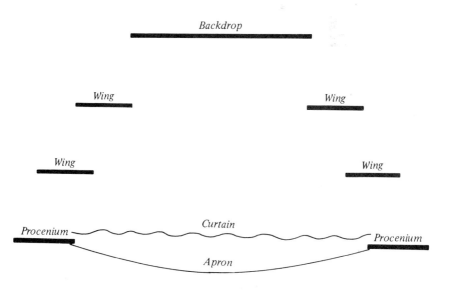

Plan of the stage.

Acting areas or "open" stages can be created in a rectangular room simply by varying the seating.

stages before, but somehow they became lost to view. Now, when most people think of a theatre, they recall immediately the proscenium, invented by Italian Renaissance painters who wanted to make their pictures move. Why European actors ever allowed themselves to be forced into the "arch" has never ceased to amaze me. The only possible reason is the ever-present one—that there is more money to be made from pictures that move than from those that don't. The picture frame conceals the elaborate machinery for changing scenes, but that tight little peephole it creates at one end of the auditorium has all but killed theatre by removing its dimension. Staying within the prosceniums of public halls, however elaborate the machinery behind them, will not help widen the frontier of drama by putting the dimension back.

If, through lack of money, groups can't create their own theatres, they can at least create their own *stages*—stages of the "open" kind which may be adjusted to suit many different kinds of plays. Later in this chapter I will explain that some plays need the proscenium arch because, like pictures, they need frames, but for the moment it is imperative to define the words "open" and "stage." In theatre, the open stage is an acting space in the same room as the auditorium. A stage, normally and strictly speaking a raised platform, can also be an acting space at floor level. There are many possible variations for an open-stage theatre, but I will talk specifically about the three most useful, and the three that fit into the most common buildings.

The end stage
has an acting area across one end of the room that also contains the auditorium. There is no proscenium arch, although a transportable one could be fitted as and when required.
The thrust stage
has an acting area against the wall of a room and the auditorium is arranged to embrace the three open sides. In fact, the stage need not be rectangular, and it is sometimes advantageous if it isn't. This is the form of the Classical Greek theatres and of the Elizabethan playhouses.
Theatre-in-the-round
has an acting area in the middle of the room, entirely surrounded by the auditorium. It seems to have been the commonest form of primitive theatre.

Look now at the detailed diagrams. They show how a hypothetical room measuring forty-two feet square could be converted into an adaptable theatre, embracing theatre-in-the-round, thrust and end stages—simply by rearranging the seating. Obviously the suggestion would have to be adjusted according to the circumstances. It might not be possible, for instance, to find accommodation with so many doors as the diagrams show, in which case the room would still function as an adaptable theatre but with limited versatility. A group planning to use the suggestion for a new building, however, would do well to have all entrances included. The adaptable theatre would then be equipped to cope with all nine schematic stage variations shown in the diagrams.

More than anything else, the hypothetical room is intended to show that drama doesn't demand exorbitant space—particularly with amateurs. All it really requires is a medium-sized room where walls, ceiling and floor can be marked by nails and splashed with paint, where spotlights can puncture darkness and pick out actors, and where imagination can freely expand in every direction. If there's enough room for the actors to act and the

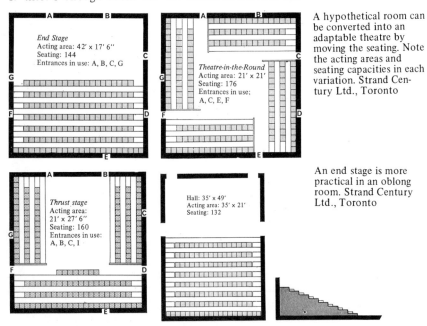

A hypothetical room can be converted into an adaptable theatre by moving the seating. Note the acting areas and seating capacities in each variation. Strand Century Ltd., Toronto

End Stage
Acting area: 42' x 17' 6"
Seating: 144
Entrances in use: A, B, C, G

Theatre-in-the-Round
Acting area: 21' x 21'
Seating: 176
Entrances in use: A, C, E, F

Thrust stage
Acting area: 21' x 27' 6"
Seating: 160
Entrances in use: A, B, C, I

Hall: 35' x 49'
Acting area: 35' x 21'
Seating: 132

An end stage is more practical in an oblong room. Strand Century Ltd., Toronto audience to sit, you've found yourself a theatre—even if it *is* the empty warehouse just around the corner, or that vacant room above the local furniture store. There's another urgent requirement, however—two johns!

Refer to the diagrams again and see what a room, forty-two feet square, can provide:

The end stage: an acting area 42 feet by 17 feet, 6 inches, seating 144
The thrust stage: an acting area 21 feet by 27 feet, 6 inches, seating 160
Theatre-in-the-round: an acting area 21 feet by 21 feet, seating 176

There are two basic requirements for any theatre: the audience must be able to see and hear the actors. This may seem so obvious as not to need stating, but these requirements are frequently ignored. While acoustics are often beyond the control of groups building a theatre on a shoestring, there is little excuse for not assuring that each member of the audience has an uninterrupted view of the action. Depending on how high it is raised and how well the seats are raked to combat it, a stage can provide an audience with an unnatural view. Raking seats is an expensive proposition, though, and is not always possible in a low building. The cheapest way of ensuring a clear view of the stage under these circumstances is by keeping the acting area at floor level—and lifting the audience. To cut costs, the first two rows could be at floor level and each subsequent row raised on portable risers. (The diagrams for the adaptable theatre provide for these to be three feet, six inches wide, seven feet long and eight inches deep.) Ideally, however, the entire audience should be above the stage.

Having a raised stage can create further hurdles. It can restrict the movability of the small items of scenery which are likely to be used. (Open theatre cannot use flats and cumbersome scenery, and thereby cuts costs.) A raised stage can also prevent overhead lighting from striking the actors at the correct angle.

When the seating has to be comprised of chairs that can be stacked, it's better if they're of the type that can be clipped side-by-side in lines of four or more. Chairs are often set too closely together; the suggested distance between centres of adjacent seats is twenty-one inches. Similarly, *rows* of seats can be too close for comfort, and the recommended leg room is at least three feet. In the three detailed diagrams, the amount of seating possible with each variation is estimated on the basis of about three feet, six inches leg room. This may be too generous for some groups wanting to accommodate larger audiences.

No matter how carefully the seating and sightlines have been calculated, the audience cannot see the actors without light. Since plays are usually presented in the evening, this means artificial light. Electricity has provided the theatre with its only really new device in the last five thousand years or so. If there is no light in the theatre, or if the lighting apparatus is improperly placed, the audience will either see nothing or only a distorted part of what they are intended to see. The facilities for hanging lights must therefore be a main concern.

There are two further general points to be stressed, no matter what form of open theatre is being planned. First, entrances into the auditorium, especially those used by the actors, should be carefully arranged in relation to light and sound. They should not let in unwanted light and noise, and actors should not be expected to go from a brilliantly-lit corridor into a darkened theatre. Light traps and acoustic barriers should be provided where necessary, but equally, an actor should not be expected to go through a soundproof door into an acting area. He has to hear his cue. Entrances to the acting area should be on the same level, and passages for the performers should be of generous dimensions.

The second point concerns storage space for chairs, risers, properties and costumes. Because the open stage will need less scenery in the way of flats, screens and solid units are likely to be used instead. Theatre-in-the-round requires good properties and costumes, by virtue of its proximity with the audience, and, since these are rare, they may have to be especially made. Ideally, when planning a theatre, provision should be made for a good wardrobe room and a workshop—both nearby.

A minor limitation which my hypothetical adaptable theatre imposes concerns stage *shapes.* Only by placing chairs individually can curved or circular acting areas be created, and these may be required for certain types of play. It's always worth remembering that acting area configuration is usually determined by the type of play most commonly produced and is based upon its requirements. A circular or elliptical stage is popular with producers offering opera or musical

114

comedy and some historical plays. A curvilinear form, as any text on the psychology of design will tell us, is most easily associated with fanciful or comic productions, or with those in which movement patterns tend to be indirect and artificial (such as mannered comedy, antique or Baroque drama, or plays with music). Since such elliptical forms and undulating curves are the distinguishing characteristics of Baroque design, a stage of this shape brings this period immediately to mind.

Occasionally the contrast between realistic straight-line movement and a curved stage is unsuitable for realistic drama for the following additional reasons:

The actors tend to rotate like fish in a bowl, developing curved movement patterns conforming to the curved edge of the stage.
On a circular stage, crosses are all of the same length, due to the constant diameter, leading to monotony in blocking or to noticeable attempts to break up the pattern.
Realistic room forms cannot be accommodated unless part of the stage is masked off, reducing the acting area, and forcing parts of the audience to view the scene across a no man's land that is not otherwise justifiable.

A rectangular stage is suitable for plays demanding a realistic outline conforming to interior architecture, but the shape is not suitable for the proper pictorial representation of non-realistic plays or for open exterior scenes, since:

The "hard" straight edge is psychologically inappropriate for fanciful drama, comedy and the natural outdoors.
The sharp corners are deep wedges into the audience seating areas, and blocking within these spaces is remote from patrons on the other side of the stage, being roughly equivalent to scenes in the proscenium theatre played close to the back wall.
A perfectly square stage is much more restrictive and forms a hard delineation between seating and acting areas.

The most important feature of open theatre generally is that it brings the emphasis of the presentation onto the actor. On the thrust stage and in the theatre-in-the-round particularly, it restores to him the dignity of being a person in three dimensions. People who are worried about theatre-in-the-round because the audience must see the actor's back are under the delusion that he only works with his front, or that he is flat—rather like the foofah sponges that arrive dried and flattened, ready for use in the bathtub. The conventions of the proscenium stage may have "flattened" the actor in this way, but soak him in water and he will fill out into a more appealing shape.

Finally, it is frequently said that *any* play can be performed on a thrust stage or in the round but with

that I cannot agree. I believe that *most* can, especially in the more modern repertoire, but there are still plays that—like pieces of art—benefit from a frame and demand the right to be viewed only from the front. Arguments as to what is meant exclusively for the proscenium will continue for a long time, which suggests

Note Michael Egan's attractive setting for this 1920's version of Jean Anouilh's *Ring Around the Moon* (staged by London Little Theatre). Beta Photos, London, Ontario

more than anything else that theatre is not born of hard and fast rules, and neither should it be if it is to retain its intrigue. However, I like to define the differences thus: a play performed in the round or on a thrust stage can receive extra dimension for which it has no use. It needs instead a depth of illusion that perhaps only the proscenium can give. Examples are plays set in drawing rooms, where the realism of the setting is an integral part of the performance. In very general terms, therefore, plays that can use the "extra rope" of the thrust stage and the theatre-in-the-round are usually those that have a setting which is secondary to the plot or theme; or else they are plays that are metaphysical, have strong elements of pageantry, or are set in the outdoors.

Reading List

Adix, Vern, *Theatre Scenecraft* (The Children's Theatre Press).

Burris-Meyer, Harold and Cole, Edward C., *Scenery for the Theatre* (Little, Brown).

Corry, Percy, *Amateur Theatrecraft* (Pitman).

Gillette, A. S., *Stage Scenery, Its Construction and Rigging* (Harper).

Melvill, Harald, *Complete Guide to Amateur Dramatics* (Rockliff).

Melvill, Harald, *Designing and Painting Scenery for the Theatre* (Rockliff).

Philippi, Herbert, *Stagecraft and Scene Design* (Houghton, Mifflin).

Selden, Samuel and Sellman, Hunton D., *Stage Scenery and Lighting* (Appleton-Century-Crofts).

Southern, Richard, *Proscenium and Sight-lines* (Faber & Faber).

Zinkeisen, Doris, *Designing for the Stage* (Studio).

11) Stage Lighting

Equipment, spotlighting, floodlighting, front-of-house, illumination, lighting on a shoestring, lighting for open stages.

When you give a lighting man his equipment you are, in effect, giving him the paint and the brushes, and he must, in turn, provide the finished canvas, through technique and artistic ability. He can, of course, be provided with advice and information on the application of his paints and how much he will need for his size of canvas, but if he's without artistic ability this will be only of meagre help. With some artistic ability it will help him proportionately more. If he's an artist he will probably ignore advice completely and go his own way to a success far greater than technique will ever give.

A basic knowledge of technique, however, is essential to all creative work, and the stage lighting man is by no means excepted.

Stage lighting performs two functions. First and foremost, it must illuminate the actor. Unless he can be seen he will not be heard, strange as that may seem, because the audience's attention will be elsewhere—probably wondering why he isn't properly lit. Even if a scene represents a darkened room or the middle of the night, the lighting man (or the electrician as he's called in some of the larger theatre companies) has to find a way of making the audience comprehend the environment and, at the same time, light the actor's face. The lighting in some amateur productions often illuminates the floor, ceiling and walls, but misses the actor's face. Every available light is simply turned on and the backstage crew stands back in the wings and hopes for the best. Needless to say, this is not the way to do it. Brilliant white light has the effect of making a stage look smaller, flattening depth and destroying colour values in costumes and settings. While the actor will be seen, he will not in any way stand out. For that moment, the dramatic illusion will have been lost.

This brings me to the second function of stage lighting—to help the actor by making the audience believe that the painted canvas flat is a solid wall, or that the light which shines through the window is a street lamp or the moon. Lighting plays an important part in a production and, used imaginatively, it can bring a performance to life. I've seen plays, however, where lighting the stage has simply meant turning on a row of overhead lights and footlights. It hasn't mattered whether the scene was taking place in a miner's oil-lit cottage or on a ship in the middle of the Atlantic Ocean. The lights were the same in both intensity and direction.

Amateurs are not always able to attain good

lighting because a number of halls and auditoriums in which they are forced to play still have old-fashioned equipment. This amounts to nothing more than a row of about eighteen sixty-watt lamps stuck up behind the proscenium arch and a row of footlights with equal intensity. The result is that the footlights cast shadows on the back of the set and there is no overhead lighting far enough back to cancel out these shadows. It's then up to the lighting man, the director and the stage manager to find alternative ways of lighting their show, and this is not always easy to do without much expense. A director should be aware of the artistic value of lighting and should know what visual effects he wants for his play. He should also know something of the way in which these can be achieved. He may have a highly-efficient stage manager and lighting man, but the director who has his own ideas for lighting commands the respect of the backstage crew.

Before talking more specifically about lights and how they may be used for maximum effect, it's important to consider where lighting the show should actually begin. Many groups rarely alter their lighting from one show to the other. They decide that just because a light was effective in a certain position for *Murder in the Red Barn,* it's going to be just as effective for *The Man Who Came to Dinner.* This is by no means the case. Each show must be planned individually. From attending rehearsals, the stage manager will be able to advise the lighting man what sections of the stage will be the most important—where the actors will be positioned at climaxes, what entrances will be used more than others (although all entrances have to be lit to justify their places on the set) and what, if any, special lighting effects will be required. The stage manager and the lighting man should always remember: it's easy to light an actor and it's easy to light the stage to give a credible picture. The challenge is how to do both at the same time.

Stage lights are divided into two main types: *spotlights,* which pick out or "spot" the actor in a localized pool of light, and *floodlights,* which flood light evenly over a much wider area. There are various sizes of floodlights, from 100 to 1,000 watt, and they are very useful for lighting the general acting area and the back-cloth. In effect, they paint in the foundation wash of light, while the spotlights provide the highlights. The angle of light from the flood can be controlled by using a hood (sometimes called a "top hat"), but a flood can never be used as a spot.

Most stage lighting, especially in the proscenium theatre, comes from above the actor's head. It's mounted on pipes (also known as "bars") which run horizontally from wing to wing. Depending upon the depth of the stage, there might be several pipes, but small stages such as those most commonly used by Little Theatre groups are usually only equipped with two or three. The No. 1 pipe is considered the most important of the lighting positions because it is farthest downstage. It should be situated as close as possible to the inside of the proscenium.

In some of the older proscenium theatres, the stage is lit additionally by footlights. Neither footlights nor lights from the pipes can be used without each other. Footlights cast upward shadows and highlights on the chin and eye sockets, and, if they are used at all, their function should be to counteract any unwanted shadows cast by overhead lighting—shadows under the eyebrows, nose and chin, Furthermore, floodlights should never be as powerful as overhead lighting. Their customary misuse is to treat them as a main source of illumination instead of a very subsidiary one. If economy is essential, the footlights should be the first sacrifice. They are better used for lighting a cyclorama at the back of the stage (to give such colourful effects as sunrise, sunset, night or day). In this case they then become known as a *cyclorama groundrow*.

Moving the footlights necessitates the use of alternative lighting from the front. Most modern theatres have replaced the footlights with front-of-house spotlights, which are an improvement, but which have to be carefully adjusted to be effective. Ideally, they should be hung so that their beams are at an angle of between thirty-five and forty-five degrees from the horizontal. A first balcony is often too low for this adjustment; a second balcony is likely to be better. Few Little Theatre groups are fortunate enough to play in theatres with balconies, so they have to find an alternative method of hanging front-of-house spots—by fixing special perches or pipes to the back wall or ceiling of the auditorium. Most front-of-house spotlights should be placed and focused so they will adequately light an actor standing near the front edge of the stage, and the best position for this is on the side walls. But this position requires sufficient height to permit the beams to be directed diagonally, thus avoiding shadows on the background. Again an angle from between thirty-five and forty-five degrees from the horizontal is usually the most satisfactory. Two spots from each side are essential. The lower one helps to correct facial shadows.

It is worth mentioning here that front-of-house spots are necessary even if footlights are being used. Footlights successfully light an actor standing five or six feet back, but, when he moves well down to the front edge of the stage, they only illuminate his legs.

There is a further direction of on-stage light: It should come diagonally so that both sides of an object, particularly an actor's face, are lit. Just as overhead lighting helps eradicate shadows cast by lights from the front, so diagonal lights ensure that an actor is illuminated when he's standing or sitting in profile. The environment in which we live is such that the sources of light are rarely equal, and an expert would suggest that spotlights should be set with their beams providing diagonal light (and, if possible, set up at slightly different heights and intensities) so there is a careful balance of shadows. We have worked so far on the assumption that shadows are unwanted. Sometimes, shadows can give depth to a picture—but only if they are in the right places!

Diagonal or directional lighting from the wings or behind the set is also required to provide other sources of light. The two main divisions, natural and artificial light, can be subdivided into: daylight in open scenes or through windows, doors and arches; night light from the moon and stars; and artificial light from chandeliers, floor, wall and table lamps, candles and fireplaces.

Let's consider how best to suggest that the apparent source of light is, in fact, the real source. Although daylight is normally diffused, it is usually accompanied, on the stage at least, by sunlight. This suggests the time of day or year, and adds atmosphere. Whether this light comes through doors, windows, trees or wings, it can be simulated with either spotlights or floodlights. If floods are used, they serve the additional purpose of lighting backings, but spots are generally to be preferred since the intensity of light and the control of the beam is greater. The direction of the light is, therefore, more marked. Whichever is used should be on offstage stands, so placed that they will give the required effect without casting the shadows of the backstage crew onto the set. The size and type of unit will depend entirely on the size of the stage but, in general, the wattage should exceed that of any other spotlights in use. Moonlight will, of course, be contrived in the same way, subject to colour and intensity. When the set is presumed to be lit from artificial light, such as lamps, it is best to cover the areas concerned with spotlights fixed to the same circuit. As an actor switches on a lamp, a spotlight comes on simultaneously. The normal position for these spots is on the No. 1 pipe.

Basically then, two kinds of lighting are needed for the stage: diffused lighting, which will light the entire acting area and the back of the set or back-cloth; and directional highlighting, that not only lights the actor but directs the audience's attention to focal points in the scene.

Now let's consider in more detail the lighting man's main units.

Spotlights
There are three basic types of spotlight, each designed with a specific job in mind. Besides providing a large range of intensities, these spots emit a wide choice of beam both in quality and spread. Their names will vary from one company to another.

The ellipsoidal spotlight (sometimes called a mirror spotlight, a profile spotlight or a leko spot) is so called because it uses an ellipsoidal reflector and a plano-convex or stepped lens. It gives a sharply-defined beam which can be controlled by shutters or an iris. Its main use is as a front-of-house spotlight. In some of the larger theatres, more powerful ellipsoidal spotlights are used as follow spots—to follow the performer around the stage.

The Fresnel spotlight is named after the inventor, Augustin Fresnel (1783-1827), whose experiments led to the development of lenses still used today in lighthouses. It uses a spherical reflector and the famous Fresnel lens, and gives a highly-efficient soft-edged beam with wide adjustability from spot focus to flood focus. All Fresnel lenses used on the stage give much more light than the plano-convex lenses they have supplanted. Furthermore, the light is softer and does not need to be frosted. However, Fresnel lenses have a tendency to emit low-intensity stray light beyond the main beam. Consequently, they should never be used in a front-of-house position. They are highly suitable for providing lighting from the wings across the stage, and to give the effect of sunlight through a window, for example. The stray light can be controlled when necessary by using a hood or barn-door attachment. Fresnel spots are also hung from the first pipe and are focused upon centre stage. Sometimes they are useful on the second pipe to light the upstage area, which is often a dead spot as far as the actor is concerned. Within the same family there is a versatile little light called a junior spot, which is relatively inexpensive. It uses a 250- or 500-watt lamp, and is in common use on the smaller stages.

The follow spotlight gives a high intensity sharp-edged beam which can be thrown into narrow- or wide-flood focus. It is generally required for brilliantly-lit productions or for any presentation in which the throw distance exceeds 100 feet, and is controlled from the back of the auditorium by an operator.

Floodlights
As I have said, floodlights are used to flood general areas of the stage with diffused lighting. Unlike spotlights, they do not have lenses. A floodlight therefore gives forth a beam with only a lamp and a reflector. They are available in two basic types:

The narrow-angled beam light projector is sometimes used as an alternative to the Fresnel spot to simulate sunlight and moonlight. Because of its almost parallel rays and very high intensity, it is often considered more efficient for this purpose. This type of floodlight, optically similar to the familiar searchlight, has been used successfully in modern techniques of backlighting.

The wide-angle ellipsoidal flood (or scoop) is used mainly for lighting backgrounds. When used to illuminate a cyclorama, it should be mounted with several others of the same type, and directed at the surface from several feet away, either from the stage floor or from a pipe. This ensures an even distribution of light.

Battens (or borderlights or striplights)
Battens are normally mounted permanently on the pipes in sectional units of eight, and are then known as compartment battens. Their job is to produce a generally shadowless illumination in a range of colours, and to serve a supplementary role on the acting area to spotlights. They are also used for toning and blending, and

for lighting backgrounds. As the efficiency of lamps, reflectors and colour media has increased, new and better battens have evolved. They are made today in a wide variety of models, either as continuous strips or in section units. However, I consider battens in striplighting form (which are really only small floods joined together) too inflexible to warrant the expense for groups working on a tight budget. Whereas spots and floods can be individually angled, battens can only be varied by their degree of tilt.

(Striplighting, incidentally, is by no means new to theatre. Early Renaissance performers were illuminated solely by rows of candles behind the top of the proscenium and along the front edge of the stage.)

Dimmers

The gradual fading in and out of the stage lights is important in creating suspense and maintaining atmosphere. Illusion is shattered if the stage is suddenly plunged into darkness, accompanied by the loud click as the blackout switch is pressed. By the use of dimmers, one colour can be imperceptibly faded out while another is brought up. There are several kinds of dimmers, but perhaps the most applicable here is the Junior-8, manufactured by the English firm of Rank Strand Electric Limited. It is sold around the world to thousands of amateur groups, mainly because it is relatively inexpensive (between $530 and $550 in North America). It is compact, transportable and easy to operate. There are, of course, many types of dimmer, which vary in price, size and complexity. Some are capable of handling up to 100 circuits or more. The Junior-8, on the other hand, has only eight circuits and four dimmers, but it is nevertheless capable of coping with most productions staged by the average Little Theatre group. Provision has been made for the addition of further circuits and dimmers, and the Junior-8 is considered a safe and sensible investment.

It's now generally recognized that even the smallest stages need a dimmer board, even if it's being used for a one-set play where the action takes place within a few hours and the lights do not therefore change much in intensity. Ideally, there should be a dimmer in each circuit, but for economic reasons this may have to be sacrificed. The cost of the dimmer board (or lighting panel, as it's sometimes called) is considerably affected by the type, the number of dimmers and circuits, and the method of controlling them.

Spots and floods are usually on separate circuits, as are any other lights that may have to be used individually, but these factors have to be decided upon when drawing up the lighting plot.

Lighting on a Shoestring

There are many heroic groups in Little Theatre for which even the most modest equipment will be unattainable. Indeed, some of them work on platforms that never begin to be stages. They need not despair, however, because on just a few dollars it's still possible to have basically efficient lighting, which yields some dramatic possibilities.

A shortage of money puts ellipsoidal spotlights for front-of-house use right out of the question and, although it's not good practice, these can be replaced by junior floods, suspended near the stage and fitted with a hood to narrow the beam and reduce spill onto the proscenium. These floods should be hung on the auditorium ceiling as near to the walls as possible, so they are directed diagonally. As there is no way of focusing them, the exact distance will have to be determined by the spread of light. If there is no proscenium, the hood can be dispensed with.

Overhead stage lighting can be provided by four more junior floods, fixed at the sides of the acting area and adjusted so their beams are directed diagonally into the middle of the stage. Even with only three junior floods it's possible to create some interesting diffused lighting.

But what about the highlighting? Since Fresnel spots might be too expensive, this would have to come from the versatile little junior spotlight which has a lamp behind in which the lens can be moved backwards and forwards to either spread or tighten the beam. Two or three junior spots clamped to the No. 1 pipe will, for the average small production, provide adequate directional light. Junior spots will also have to be used to simulate such effects as the sun and the moon.

Lighting equipment is undeniably expensive to buy, which is why it should be purchased with care and thought. Rank Strand Electric Limited and its subsidiary companies publish several useful pamphlets on stage lighting, and are ready to give useful advice. It's also possible to hire equipment from Strand and other companies which specialize in theatrical lighting. Finally, one of the lighting man's oldest tricks is to make floodlights by setting 200-watt bulbs in large tin lids. If he's knowledgeable, the tin-lid flood can prove an asset. If, however, he's a complete novice, the device can become a fire hazard.

Lighting the Open Stage

Open stage theatre can only be concerned with tight lighting—lighting that must be concentrated solely on the acting area, without being allowed to spill into the audience sitting close by. Tight lighting, as we've discussed, comes from spots, and since floods and battens emit diffused lighting they therefore have no application. From this it may be assumed that lighting the open stage can be less expensive than lighting the proscenium. The assumption may be true, but, equally, it's by no means easier, and calls for more precision in the adjustment of the comparatively few lights it will use.

In the proscenium theatre, the lighting man has a twofold job: to light or "spot" the actor with his spotlights, and to use his diffused lighting to illuminate the set, playing area and/or back-cloth. Since open stage theatre places the emphasis on the actor and is invariably played without an elaborate set—especially in the theatre-in-the-round—the necessity for general, diffused lighting is removed. The lighting man is therefore only asked to light the actor, and light him he must—wherever he moves.

In smaller open theatres, the lights cannot afford to have the harshness of either the ellipsoidal or follow spot, or the softness of a flood, and the lighting man has to strike a balance somewhere in between. Ellipsoidal and follow spots have a place in large open theatres, like the Shakespearean Theatre in Stratford, Ontario, but in the intimate open theatre they are too intense. The alternative that comes to mind is the Fresnel spotlight, the main characteristic of which is a diffused edge to a tight beam. A number of these placed strategically around the acting area provide a clean, even wash of light that can be controlled with relative simplicity.

Because the audience sits in close proximity, only a limited amount of overhead lighting can be safely used, and most of the illumination has to come from well back in the auditorium. This leads to the lighting man's major hazard—how to light the theatre-in-the-round and the thrust stage from each of its sides. Experiment can only provide the solution but it is generally accepted that the beam of a Fresnel spot, even with its diffused edge, can be adjusted to provide the right amount of light if it strikes the actor at about forty-five degrees from the horizontal. Problems may arise if the angle is more or less:

At fifty degrees from the horizontal, unwanted shadows begin to form, particularly around the actor's eyes.

At twenty-five or thirty degrees from the horizontal, it may be difficult to keep direct light out of the eyes of members of the audience viewing from the opposite side.

In some smaller open theatres the correct angle of the beam may only be attained by having the Fresnel spots on the ceiling near the outer walls of the auditorium.

It's worth talking more about shadows. In the proscenium theatre, where the audience has to sprawl on only one side of the action, shadows distort the actor's facial expressions for too many people—especially those in the last few rows. In the open theatre, patrons in the last few rows are still relatively close to the stage and will see the actor's face clearly even *with* the shadows. Provided these are not overworked, they can be tremendously useful. The stabbing light from a few spots often has the intensity of drama that is missing from numerous and more powerful instruments, the brilliancy of which must compete with an illuminated background of scenery.

Furthermore, lighting for the open stage does not demand the use of colour filters to the extent common in the proscenium theatre. Colour in the theatre serves to emphasize the solidity of three-dimensional objects, including actors. But when an audience is sitting on three or four sides of a play, this dimension can hardly be in doubt. Colour may, of course, be used, and for special effects it may be demanded, but the entire scheme will not depend on it.

Reading List
Bentham, Frederick, *Stage Lighting* (Pitman).
Corry, Percy, *Lighting the Stage* (Pitman).
Joseph, Stephen, *Planning for New Forms of Theatre* (Rank Strand Electric).
Ost, Geoffrey, *Stage Lighting* (Herbert Jenkins).

1. Junior floods for overhead diffused lighting, pointing diagonally inwards.
2. Two more junior floods for front-of-house illumination.
3. Two junior spots on the No. 1 Pipe. More could be added.

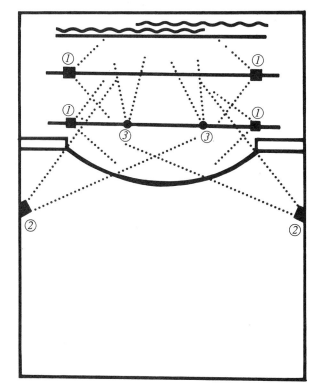

1. Junior spot
2. Fresnel spot
3. Profile spot
4. Stage flood
5. Flood with masking hood
6. Batten

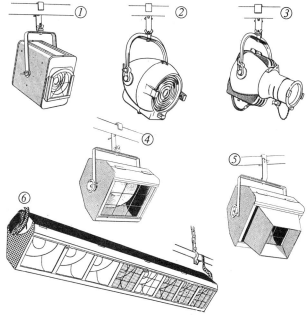

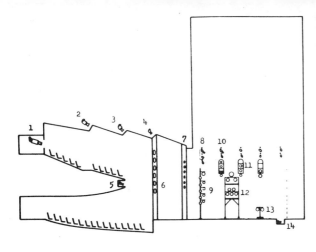

Side elevation view of theatre

Front of house
1. Booth
2. Ceiling slot, long throw
3. Ceiling slot, medium throw
4. Ceiling slot, short throw
5. Balcony front
6. Wall slot
7. Proscenium wall slot

On stage
8. Teaser position
9. Tormentor position
10. Border position
11. Ladder
12. Tower
13. Portable stands
14. Cyclorama pit

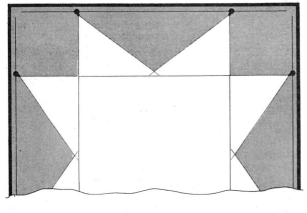

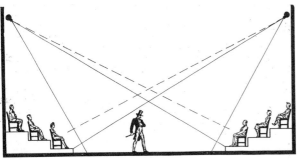

Note this complete and relatively inexpensive illumination of theatre-in-the-round with eight Fresnel spotlights. Above: suggested positioning of the lights. Below: how acting area is covered. The maximum advisable beam elevation is dotted (it is directed at laps in the front row). Strand Century Ltd., Toronto

The principles and vary-
ing capabilities of lights.
Strand Century Ltd.,
Toronto

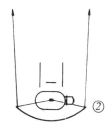

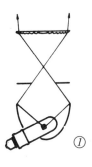

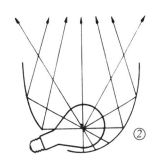

①
Ellipsoidal spotlights

②
Floodlights

③
Follow–spot lights

④
Fresnel spotlights

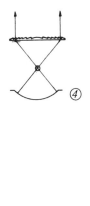

12) Sound

On tape, on effects records, manual simulations, cues, the sound man at rehearsals.

A friend of mine who lusted after sound effects wanted to reproduce a huge bomber aircraft for a play in which he had the lead. One Sunday afternoon in early spring found him bent over the wheel of his little Japanese car with a portable tape recorder tucked inside the glove compartment. At seventy miles an hour, he decided, his bomber sounded like a spitfire. At eighty miles an hour there was an improvement, but the simulation was still not good enough. At ninety miles an hour he got a speeding ticket, went to court and lost his licence. Ironically, the sound man decreed his tape was too muffled anyway—and used an effects record.

Whether or not the sound man was right is hard to judge without hearing my friend's tape, but one thing is certain: the necessity for ingenuity in sound effects has been largely removed by the invention of recordings on which it's possible to find almost everything—from the cuckoo's first song in spring and the cry of a baby, to the sounds of a battalion marching to war and the stutter of a pneumatic drill.

So it transpires that most plays don't now require the services of a "noises off" man. Once, one of theatre's backstage stalwarts, he was given such chores as trotting two halves of a coconut shell against an offstage wall as the highwayman rode past the cottage, or producing the sound of surf by rolling a pound-and-a-half of dried peas around the inside of a cardboard box or drum. Today, it's the line of least resistance to turn to records and a tape recorder, even though there are more ingenious substitutes. Indeed, some of the effects produced manually from the wings are still considered better than recordings, because they are believable to the audience. The tape recorder and the record—even in view of the perfection they have enjoyed in recent years—still manage to produce a "canned" impression of some sounds. Doorbells and ringing telephones, for instance, lose their clarity on record or tape. These are best simulated by a battery-powered bell unit with a push button—something that can be made inexpensively and is guaranteed to work, despite constant use. It's also possible to have an ordinary telephone wired so that it can be made to ring by a push button. Many sounds, however, including hurdy-gurdies, carousels, bagpipes played collectively, carillon chimes, cathedral bells, fanfares and very large crowds virtually have to be recorded.

Recordings, of course, have proved to be an asset to the theatre and will continue to be so—but only if they are used intelligently and with finesse. I've heard sounds of baby sparrows come across the auditorium like seagulls before a storm; distant trains have thundered past only a few feet away. Equally, an illusion (and theatre is made of illusion, remember) has been snapped by the click of the tape recorder switch. I've even sat in an audience and heard the sound man running his tape backwards and forwards trying to find his next cue. In one of my early productions, I recall with embarrassment, the sound man pushed down his button to produce the slow, reverent toll of the bell of St. Anthony's Church, which he'd spent three Sunday mornings recording—and the toilet flushed! Laugh if you like, but it can have a numbing effect upon the actors. How the throaty flush of the sound man's toilet ever found its way into *Murder in the Red Barn,* I'll never know. It was probably left over from the previous play, *The Odd Couple.*

This brings me to the sound man's first undertaking: he must see that his tape is clean and in good condition, and that as far as he can tell it is not likely to break. He must then read the script thoroughly and note what effects are wanted by the author. By attending rehearsals and production meetings he will also become familiar with those effects the director has decided to omit. The sound man must then produce a tape of all effects that need to be recorded, and compile a sound cue form which will show at a quick glance the specific line or action at which the sound must be brought into use. The length of the effect should also be shown, the amount of volume required for it, and the line on which it should either cut off abruptly or be faded out. The sound man must see that his effects are on tape in the order in which they will be used. He must also make arrangements for manual simulations that will be created offstage, and have these on a separate list—a manual sound cue form. It goes without saying that the manner in which these effects are to be produced should be decided upon early and not left until the last minute.

To avoid confusion during performances, each effect should be recorded at the same speed. It is imperative for the tape to be completed at least three weeks before opening night, so sound may be incorporated into rehearsals. Just as the actor likes to practise critical moments in his scenes, so the sound man should want to practise his critical moments. Sound cues are indeed critical, otherwise they wouldn't be in the script.

Split-second timing with cues is as important to the pace and believability of the play as seeing that sound doesn't burst in between the lines, unless it is of the kind that virtually has to. Equally, there are many kinds of sound that have to be carefully and skilfully faded in, coinciding perhaps with the fading of lights and the movements of an actor. At the end of my production of *No Exit,* for instance, I ordered a fifteen-second fade-out of the lights and an eight-second fade-in with taped music. The two had to fit well together lest the final moments of the play should be cast into the sink.

By the same token, many directors in amateur theatre are preoccupied with sound. Every effect must be included, however formidable the job of producing it, however great the chances that it will be slovenly executed, and however relatively unimportant it may be to the play. (Do we always have to hear the doctor's car pull up outside the house when a ring at the doorbell will do? Do we have to hear the maid drop the coffeepot in the kitchen when her next entrance line is, "I'm sorry, Ma'am, but I've just broken your prize possession—the coffeepot.") I believe that theatre's main concerns are the visual aspect and the spoken word, and it's sometimes preferable to let the imagination of the audience supply many of the sound effects.

Sound effects records are more expensive than ordinary records because the fee charged for them includes the performing licence. Anyway, they are not always a good investment for the Little Theatre group working on a shoestring. Used once, they are invariably stored away and are seldom, if ever, needed again. Necessity, they say, is the mother of invention. Invention, in turn, calls for ingenuity. Ingenuity will, perhaps, lead to the discovery of many ways to create authentic-sounding effects. Indeed, there must be more which could be added to this humble list:

Airplanes
Plenty of recordings are available. A poor substitute, however, is an electromagnetic vibrator with its arm held against a drum.

Animal Noises
Cow and frog noises can be produced by various musical instruments, in particular by the saxophone and the oboe. The human voice is also effective if cleverly used. The roar of a lion is accurately imitated by drawing taut a string attached to the inside of a metal bucket or can.

The string should be treated with resin and rubbed with a leather glove.

Bomb Explosions

Fire a shotgun, using a blank cartridge, into a metal can or barrel. By wrapping the can in a blanket or carpet, the quality of sound may be changed. (See Explosions.)

Birds

Find a human bird-whistler, or talk to the owner of the local novelty store. He probably has a supply of children's whistles that imitate birds sufficiently well. Records are not always effective unless the bird noises are distant.

Cars

Plenty of recordings are available of cars starting, idling, moving, skidding and crashing. An electric egg beater with its tip held against the bottom of a can gives an authentic engine sound. An electric vibrator may also be used.

Crashes

Drop a box of broken glass. For metallic crashes, drop a box of scrap metal.

Crowd Noises

The most effective of "noises off," if done well, are the offstage crowd voices. The live voice sounds so much better than the "canned" one. Yet of all "noises off," these are the ones which so often fail most dismally. Scenes of wild enthusiasm portrayed offstage by a few straggling voices crying, "Rhubarb!" can never be anything but laughable. The director should rehearse his crowd offstage just as much as the rest of his actors, and on the night of the production there should be a conductor in charge of the crowd. Apart from the question of superiority of tone of the live voice over the mechanical one, there is the added advantage of being able to increase and decrease volume and pace, to build to a climax at the right moment, and to time bursts of applause on given speeches. None of this can be done on tape or record. If an "effects chorus" is not available, a few voices *plus* an effects record will add to the authenticity of the sound.

Crunching Sound

Try walking on a large box filled with flake glue and covered with a cloth.

Door Slam

Find a real door, or slap a short length of one-by-three on the floor. Recordings do not capture an accurate sound.

Explosions

For a loud explosion, a firework may be used. This must be electrically detonated in a large tin bathtub covered with fine wire netting to contain flying pieces. A can whacked on a drum will give the sound of a small explosion, and I have found that carefully rehearsed hand claps are quite successful for firework "crackers."

Fighting

Punch a padded surface close to a tape recorder microphone. The sound of a body being beaten can be effected by striking a watermelon with a stick.

Fire

Twist or crush cellophane close to the microphone. (See Crunching Sound.)

Hail

See Rain.

Horses' Hoofs

There's no mystery about this effect. Nearly everyone knows about the coconut shells. In order to manipulate the shells easily, however, straps should be attached to them, through which the hands can be slipped. The shells can then be trotted on a hard surface or against each other. If the horse is galloping on turf, a felt pad on top of a hard surface will give the right sound. Plastic mugs can be used as an alternative to coconut shells.

Locomotive

The sound is best created by rubbing sandpaper blocks together. A stronger locomotive effect is produced by striking sheet metal with a wire duster. A snare drum may also be used. Many good recordings are available.

Machine Gun

Hold a couple of wooden slats to the spokes of a quickly revolving wheel.

Pain

Fetch the stage manager's ankles a hefty wallop with a shillelagh!

Rain

A "rain box" is quite easy to make. All that is needed is a box about a yard long and eight inches wide, preferably made of thin plywood. The box is divided into three, by partitions nine inches apart. Large holes, an inch in diameter, are then made in the partitions. Dried peas are put into one end of the box and the lid is securely fastened. If the box is tilted up at one end, the peas will filter through the holes and will imitate the sound of rain. When all the peas have dropped through to the other end, the box can be tilted the reverse way. (See Wind.)

Shots
Genuine revolver or gun shots are needed if the sound
warrants intensity. Always use blank cartridges.
Squeak
Rub a resin-coated rag on a glossy surface, or twist a
wooden peg within a hole of similar diameter. Try twist-
ing a moist cork in a bottle.
Steam
Release air from a tank or tire. Most service stations have
air under pressure in guns.
Surf
Roll dried peas in a cardboard box or on a drum. A
coarse scrubbing brush rubbed over an oven tin also
makes a good noise—especially if a garden roller is
trundled backstage at the same time.
Thunder
One of the sound man's best friends is a thunder sheet—a
sheet of thin sheet metal about three feet by six feet,
which is very effective when hung up and shaken. Experiment is needed here. Depending on how the sheet is
shaken, the thunder will be either violent or subdued.
Thunder, incidentally, is hard to record accurately.
Wind
Wind is required on stage probably more than any other
effect, so it's worthwhile possessing a wind machine.
This consists of two circles of wood joined together in a
cylindrical shape by slats of wood about an inch apart. A
handle is fixed to one end so that the cylinder may be
rotated. It must also be supported on a trestle, or in a
frame with a crossbar on one side. A strip of sailcloth or
canvas should be stretched taut over the cylinder, one
end of which must be tacked on the crossbar and the
other end left free, but weighted. As the cylinder
rotates, the slats will rub against the canvas and produce
a whirring sound. By varying the speed of the rotation
it's possible to get anything from a moderate gust of
wind to a full-sized gale.

Reading List
Bradbury, A. J. and Howard, W. R. B., *Stagecraft* (Jenkins).
Napier, Frank, *Noises Off* (Garnet Miller).
Stewart, Hal D., *Stagecraft* (Pitman).

13) Costumes

The Little Theatre wardrobe, colour, styles, lighting, costumes on a shoestring.

Twenty centuries of historic costumes should, ideally, be documented with pictures alone. Only the words of the historians, with whom I feel hopelessly inadequate to compete, could possibly be relevant. There's still much to be said, however, on how costumes affect theatre. This I will do by showing perhaps the most practical way of compiling a Little Theatre wardrobe, and by stressing a necessity for a loyalty to the past.

The best and often only really good information on historical dress comes from books not primarily concerned with costumes: travel diaries, memoirs, account books, some novels, works on archaeology and histories of civilizations and their arts. These are the true authorities, and their value as such should never be undermined. Authenticity without necessarily a profound literalism is, I believe, the challenge history presents to theatre and this can only be accomplished by an archaeological approach which, unfortunately, is often belittled. But without it, history ceases to be history in the theatrical sense. It's therefore generally disastrous to embark on planning costumes with only a superficial knowledge of the era involved.

Whatever the era, there are two basic principles to remember when costuming a play. The first arises from the very rudimentary premise that audiences respond mostly to that which appeals to the eye. A bad gesture or clumsy movement, an ugly colour or shouting tint—these, and similar distractions, jar the visual sense. It's therefore necessary that costumes should create, individually and as a whole, a harmonious picture. This does not mean that colour schemes should always be pleasing or soothing. On the contrary, harmony serves much more than to induce the eyes and ears into a daze of appreciation. I mean that, when a cast is costumed, the colours and the cut of clothes should be so arranged that they serve a unity of purpose.

The second principle of good costuming is that it should not only be harmonious in itself, but must be capable of constructing the required atmosphere for the play—its period, its mood and style. Now it should be seen why the responsibility of providing any stage costume should *on no account* be left with the individual actor, but must be the sole undertaking of an appointed designer who views the play as an entity unto itself. This recommendation applies more particularly to modern plays—and, indeed, modern plays have to be "costumed" like any other—when actors and actresses are asked to turn up in their ugliest, smartest, flimsiest, oldest or most untidy suits or dresses. It applies even more strenuously to the young *ingénue* who has a striking new evening gown. She's not likely to concern herself with what other people might be wearing—so long as the world sees her gown! Dare I add that Little Theatre is full of such personalities.

Every Little Theatre group with serious plans to incorporate an historical play in its yearly repertoire will eventually need its own wardrobe. This, needless to say, should be organized with meticulous care, and not by the haphazard accumulation of everything and anything. Initially the wardrobe may only occupy two closets in someone's basement, but as it expands, and expand it will, it will require a rack for every period, and suitable facilities for storing accessories—hats, shoes, gloves and many other items that complete a costume. It will also need plenty of nearby working space, preferably with shelves to hold equipment, and a sink. Above all, it will require an administrator, for it goes without saying that left to the tender mercies of everyone and anyone (as is often the case) the wardrobe will persistently look like The Wreck of the Hesperus!

A wardrobe mistress must then be appointed, preferably permanently, or by the year, to be in full command to see that the costume department is afforded the dignity deserved by all who work there. One of her first jobs will be to take an inventory of all items of costume from suits, coats and dresses right down to hats, shoes and garters. With help, she must then see that this inventory is maintained, and that all that's borrowed is returned. In addition to her organizing abilities and her natural tidiness she should, ostensibly, possess other qualities: a love of history (if not a knowledge of the field), a lust for research and, above all, an eye for seeing that, with a stitch or two, some alternative buttons and a dash of jewellery, the dullest, most uninteresting blouse might be converted into something exquisitely elegant. It would be useful if her initial aim were to gather a selection of fairly adaptable costumes—gowns that by virtue of three or four pairs of detachable sleeves could be used for as many eras, and men's tailed, morning, afternoon and evening suits. By interchanging the trousers and jackets, it's possible to costume a variety of theatre's prototypes, from the most affluent of gentlemen to those who serve them—butlers, chauffeurs, batmen and commissionaires. Of course, the combination can only be effected with an assortment of accessories—black and white bow ties, cravats and vests (waistcoats), and ordinary silver ties, not to mention gloves and black shoes.

Beggars, they say, cannot be choosers. Many Little Theatre groups, by their own admission, are beggars. When setting up a wardrobe it's useful to know who in the neighbourhood is discarding what, and it's essential to have the courage to go and ask for it. Sometimes it's useful to have the courage to ask for it even if it's *not* being discarded! It's even worth placing an inexpensive advertisement in the local newspaper—"THEATRE GROUP WILL TAKE OLD CLOTHES"—because it's surprising how a patch, a seam or two and some starch and dye can subject some of the most dilapidated garments to uncanny transformations. People are hoarders by nature. That may sound sweeping, but each one of us, almost without exception, is guilty of clinging to bedspreads we'll never use, or white collarless shirts that slipped out of fashion some time ago. We hoard them

Garden City Productions (of St. Catharines, Ontario) costumed *Guys and Dolls* well. Randolph Rhodes thinking that one day they will come back into fashion. They may indeed, but by the time they do, they may have fed a hundred moths.

A persuasive tongue can convince people to part with all kinds of things—bedspreads, curtains, sheets, pillowcases, cushion covers, blankets, dressing gowns, housecoats and uncut lengths of material, which should be accepted joyfully. Dark material that may at first appear drab can, stencilled with gold and silver paint, be turned into beautiful expensive-looking brocade. Left plain, it still has a thousand uses because theatre needs dull fabrics as it does bright, happy fabrics.

Old sheets, white or otherwise, may yield enough good material for tunics and gowns for Greek and medieval plays. Blankets make exceptionally good cloaks because the material is heavy and falls well, and woollen dressing gowns can be unpicked at the seams and re-assembled inside-out as robes. Discarded evening gowns, cotton or flannelette night dresses, and out-of-date petti-coats and slips can, with minimum alteration, become part of the 1920's, a particularly difficult era to costume. Butter muslin, too, is useful for Victorian blouses and all kinds of draped head gear.

Hats should never be turned away because they can so easily be adapted with a bow, a flower or a piece of jewellery. And men's hats, while they're not quite so versatile, are also worth collecting. Boaters, berets, genuine top hats and trilbies are becoming scarce. It's worth noting here that most eras in history, particularly Victorian and Elizabethan times, are recognizable almost exclusively by their head gear. Victorian men wore top hats mostly, and peaked caps; the women wore an assortment of head pieces from bonnets to monstrosities resembling bird's nests and cabbages. Some of the most ornate hats in history, however, adorned the heads of Elizabethan men, and I've seen these made from shower caps and head gear that women wore only a few years ago. It's surprising what can be done to a hat with a needle and thread, a hot iron—and a feather!

Long-sleeved, high-necked men's and women's sweaters and cardigans will prove invaluable to the Little Theatre wardrobe, which has to comprise fairly adapt-able costumes. So, too, will plastic doilies and tray cloths, used to simulate lace for trimmings. And don't forget shoes, many types of which can be decorated with buttons, bows and buckles.

Indeed, the illusion of theatre is carried un-

Overleaf:

The costumes were well-designed for this amateur production of Jean. Girandoux's *The Mad Woman of Chaillôt.* Randolph Rhodes

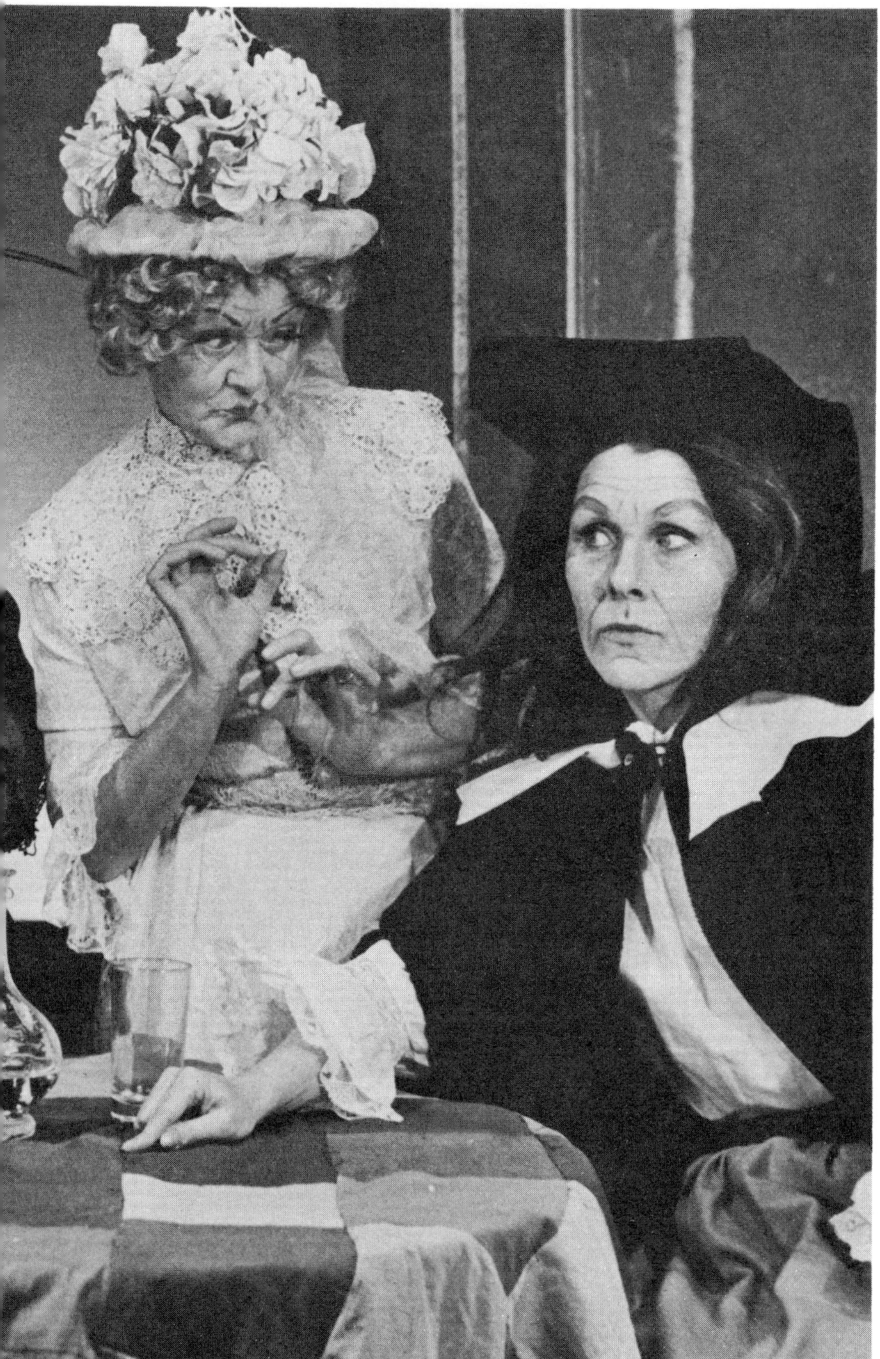

Roman   Early Soldier   Viking.   Mediaeval Peasant

Old countryman   Victorian Man   Victorian Woman

Puritan Man   Puritan woman   Elizabethan Man and Woman

compromisingly into costumes. If an actress is wearing a gown made from a blanket or a housecoat, and it looks from the audience like a garment of rich, expensive brocade, that's all that really matters. Furnishing fabrics and household linens are generally much better for period costumes though, and a good deal cheaper than ordinary dress materials which are too flimsy and often too contemporary in design. (Avoid shiny silks and satins at all cost. They look tatty under lights.)

Velvet, of course, looks beautiful on stage, but it's better to use furnishing velvet for costumes because it's heavier and less expensive than the velvet normally used for dresses. Furnishing damask is also highly suitable for rich-looking costumes, and soft woollen fabrics fall in graceful folds. One of the most obliging and effective of all materials is unbleached calico because it can be dyed or painted with poster paint, which can be washed out. It can also be kept white and used for cuffs and hats worn in Puritan times. Offers of lace curtains should never be rejected, either. These can be starched or dyed and ultimately turned into magnificent blouses and full-length dresses.

Old towels (especially the larger bath towels) and lengths of terry cloth make excellent tunics for Roman soldiers. Sacking (burlap), hessian canvas and other rugged fabrics will be needed for crude, coarse tunics, tabards and various other over-garments worn by soldiers and peasants in the Dark Ages and medieval times. These latter fabrics also absorb paint well.

When painting and dying, by the way, always remember that colours have to be strong and bold to withstand stage lighting. Pastel shades fade and tend to look insipid. This brings me to lighting, which affects the appearance of costumes more than anything else. In evolving a costume scheme, the designer *must* take the lighting plot into consideration. Ostensibly, to save time and money, she should know what colours are to be used before asking the wardrobe mistress to order materials or alter existing costumes.

Here's the general rule:

Colour of Light	Effect on Materials
Middle Pink	Bad for greens
Light Pink	Good for all colours except greens
Salmon Pink	Tends to darken blues
Dark Pink	Same as above, but more pronounced. Turns blues to purple; turns greens to blue

Lavender	Flattering; preserves and heightens natural shades
Dark Amber	Completely spoils greens and blues. Poor for reds
Light and Dark Red	Turns yellows to orange or red. Bad for greens and blues. Good for reds
Magenta	A useful vivid colour. Will bring out blues and purples. All light colours are completely wiped out
Violet	Spoils most colours as colours, but often produces new and pleasing ones, as in the case of greens. Good for some reds
New Blue	Darkens some reds
Middle Blue	Spoils no colours. Good for some
Dark Blue	Good for most colours. Tendency to turn red to black. Used for general lighting or moonlight scenes
Purple	Bad for greens. Good for reds and blues
Dark Green	Spoils all colours except green Seldom used in acting area
Light Green or Moonlight Green	Good with all colours, especially greens

This general rule can only serve to reemphasize the impossibility of permitting individual actors to choose their own costumes. Only the director is capable of creating a unity of mood out of the settings, the actors and their costumes, and his must be the guiding hand.

Every period in history has its own characteristic costumes with which, it goes without saying, it is the most integral part of a designer's job to become familiar. To know them all would take more than a lifetime because some eras were not consistent, and there are European, Middle Eastern and Asiatic influences to consider, too. Let's talk for the moment about some shapes and styles and how these can be met by amateurs.

Greek clothes with their columnar, draped look are extremely simple, and require a minimum of sewing. But there's a trap: this simplicity often makes for monotony. It's imperative, therefore, for the entire costume plan to be worked out with extra care, especially if there are to be many people in the cast, so that costumes are always visually interesting and varied within the historical confines laid down. Greek garments are generally cut on a rectangular principle and the main sewing merely entails joining seams. Pictures reveal quite clearly that men and women dressed alike. The cloak, or chlamys, as it's called by the historians, formed the basis of their wardrobes, and they also wore chitons, a type of skirt. The woman's was floor-length; the man's stopped about two inches or so beneath the knee. Additionally, women sometimes wore an over-dress, or peplos, over this chiton.

Splashes of colour can be added with pieces of carefully chosen stage jewellery, made by spraying or painting virtually anything: tin lids, corks, pieces of chain, ironmongery, old belts and ornate buttons. Many other articles could be utilized, so it's worth keeping a box handy in which to put them as they're found. It must also be said, however, that a poorly-designed costume will not be improved by overloading it with trinkets and ill-assorted pieces of finery. To be at its most effective, jewellery has to be used sparingly.

Greek theatre also requires yards of rope, cord or braid with which to girdle costumes. It also uses old sandals and these *must* be heelless. Simple Greek footwear can be made by cutting a sole from thick industrial felt, and sewing on loops through which tape may be threaded and ultimately wound up to the knees.

Costumes worn by the Romans, peasants and soldiers through the Dark Ages and on up to the Middle Ages can be tailored, too, with relatively little work. Again the cut is square.

Like Greek drama, medieval theatre utilizes materials that can be easily draped. Bolton sheeting, which is a cotton with a twill weave, is considered one of the best. An added advantage is that it easily absorbs dye. Soft wool is useful, but this is more expensive. Old sheets and blankets can also be used. Men's clothes of this period incorporate the use of such materials as felt, hessian and Bolton sheeting. For peasant characters, as I've already said, it's wise to make good use of materials with a coarse, heavy texture. Rough towelling, lightweight canvas (although this is sometimes too stiff to fall well until it's been washed several times), and sacking (burlap) are particularly satisfactory.

The universal head gear for women in medieval times was the wimple, the main purpose of which was to hide the hair. Some peasant women, however, wore men's hoods while working in the fields. A few hoods would therefore not only be perfectly permissible, but convenient in crowd scenes. The wimple is rather difficult for the actress to put on without the supervision of the wardrobe mistress, and if there are more than twenty women in the cast the job becomes tiring. A nun from a nearby convent might be able to demonstrate the fixing of a wimple. There were, in fact, several different types of medieval hats. Apart from hoods and wimples, there were chaperons, pixie and bag hats worn by men, while some women fixed two cone-like objects beneath veils.

It's interesting to note that because men emulated monks, trousers were missing during the larger part of the medieval era, and did not reappear until around the fifteenth century when the power of the Church either waned or was met by other forces. Referring to pictures again, it can be seen that the medieval era was one of nun-like women, cloaks, hoods, tabards, tunics and sleeveless jackets. Both sexes, like the Greeks, wore skirts which they draped up at either the back or the side while at work.

Whereas Greek and medieval costumes are uncomplicated in cut and depend almost exclusively on simple drapery, the Elizabethan dress is highly intricate and can be simulated with reasonable accuracy only after an exceptionally diligent study of styles, which were highly ornamental to say the least. Groups wanting to perform the plays of Shakespeare in Elizabethan dress may find it virtually impossible to be consistent with styles and will therefore have to make some compromises.

The artificial and padded shape of the Elizabethan begins in the underclothes, and unless these are properly made no amount of elaborate costume worn on top will give an authentic look. To swell their skirts, women wore hip pads, hip rolls or *farthingales,* which gave a crinolined effect. The pads and rolls are simply made from calico and stuffed with foam rubber. A child's plastic or wooden hoop can be used as a farthingale, but it will have to be positioned by a special foundation. Men, too, wore padding—under their breeches to swell their hips and the top part of their thighs. Making special pads for men will entail too much senseless work, especially if the cast is large, so it's worth knowing that the effect can be adequately given by sewing foam rubber onto the legs of swimming trunks or boxer shorts.

Generally, the Elizabethan era demands well-cut clothes from such materials as felt, canvas, blazer cloth (heavy flannel), and even suede. The Greeks tended to be drab (although on stage it's permissible to cheat with more appealing shades) but the Elizabethans wore bright, subtle, well-matched colours. Sweaters and cardigans are a vital part of the Elizabethan section of the amateur theatrical wardrobe—but not dull, thick ones, although any Elizabethan costume can be enlivened later with braids, ribbons and strips of coloured felt. Ruffs can be made from doilies, and all modern shoes (preferably suede) can be adapted with buckles and rosettes, which were also worn on garters by the more elegant Elizabethan men.

Costumes on a Shoestring
Low funds may prevent some of the more elaborate, authentic costumes from being made. Here's how an assortment of prototype theatre characters may be dressed on a shoestring.

Roman Soldier
An old sheet makes his one big item—a chiton, fastened over his left shoulder, leaving the right one bare. Round his middle he wears a simple belt of canvas or webbing. Sandals form his footwear, and a rope circlet his headdress.

Viking
Pyjama trousers and a thick, turtle-neck sweater are useful here. He also wears a canvas tabard with two or three webbing straps securing it on either side. His pyjama trousers are drawn together by strings above the ankles, and he wears woollen socks and sandals. With a horned headdress, a sword, and a garbage can lid (painted) for a shield, he looks reasonably authentic.

Old Countryman (seventeenth and eighteenth century)
He wears a knee-length, full-sleeved smock made from an old curtain or a sheet, corduroy trousers gathered with string at the ankles, and old leather boots. Give him a bright neckerchief, a felt hat, a rustic walking stick and a clay pipe.

Medieval Peasant
He is fitted out inexpensively in a tunic made from old sacks, tied around the middle with a piece of rope. Beneath the girdle he wears a thick, chunky long-sleeved sweater or jersey. This can be a turtle-neck or a

mock-turtle-neck garment. The neck is covered anyway because, on his head, the medieval peasant wears a woollen balaclava or, as an alternative, a woollen ski cap. His legs are bare, except for string wound between the ankle and the knee. On his feet: nothing.

Early Soldier
His legs are covered with thigh-length stockings knitted from string. He wears a quarter-sleeve tunic to mid-thigh, and this can be made from a tapestry curtain or bed-spread. A tabard of sacking fits over his head and is open at each side. The early soldier needs a wide leather belt. The balaclava used by the medieval peasant can be used again here, but the early soldier would wear a helmet, too. This looks rather like half a lemon, as the history books will reveal, and can be made from papier-mâché. The early soldier wears *thick* woollen socks.

Bishop
He, too, is simple to dress. His full-length, half-sleeve robe is made from old sheets or curtains, and he wears an ornamental chasuble made from hessian (burlap), which can be easily painted. The Bishop wears woollen socks *over* sneakers and his mitre can be made from cardboard.

Monk
His robe is similar to that worn by the Bishop. His long, tabard-like over-garment is made simply from a sheet. The monk wears a girdle of rope, toeless sandals, and a hood which is nothing more than a bag opened on one side.

Elizabethan Lady
She wears a long-sleeved, turtle-neck jumper of light-weight wool, a farthingale made from a child's hoop, and a long skirt made from a curtain or a sheet. There should be a striking design on the front of the dress and a ruff around the neck because the Elizabethan era was pre-occupied with ornamentation.

Elizabethan Man
He, too, wears a long-sleeved, turtle-neck jumper of light-weight wool. He also wears tights, a sleeveless ascot without a collar, made from canvas or another stiff fabric, and a ruff. The insignia of a well-dressed Elizabethan are his garters with rosettes and his hat (which will need researching).

Puritan Woman

She has a Dutch look about her, except that she's rather dowdy. Dress her in a long-sleeved, round-necked, light-weight woollen sweater, a full-length gathered skirt made from a dark curtain, thick wool stockings, calico collar and cuffs and cap (an ordinary nursemaid's cap will do), and black walking shoes with large buckles. The Puritan woman also wears a padded roll under her skirt to swell it at the hips, and a very simple apron.

Puritan Man

Give him a long-sleeved, round-necked sweater. Tuck his dark trousers into dark socks that stop two or three inches below the knee, and make him a three-quarter-length cloak from a blanket or heavy curtain. His attire is completed by a wide, calico collar (worn over the cloak), black walking shoes with large buckles, and a Puritan hat (which can be shaped with cardboard).

Victorian Man

Striped, narrow, *cuffless* trousers, fitting neatly above elastic-sided boots, and a knee-length cape are the main features of his dress. He also needs gloves, a scarf and a top hat. Victorian men were generally very well-tailored.

Victorian Woman

She needs a full, gathered skirt, a cotton print blouse, a woollen shawl, a ribboned bonnet and gloves. These items are not difficult to find. However, colours and the cut of the clothes are important here. Doilies and odd pieces of lace can be used to trim modern dresses and blouses, thus making them suitable for the Victorian woman.

Reading List

Barton, Lucy, *Historic Costumes for the Stage* (A. & C. Black).
Barton, Lucy, *History of Costume for the Stage* (Walter H. Baker).
Hansen, Henny H., *Costume Cavalcade* (Methuen).
Jackson, Sheila, *Simple Stage Costumes and How to Make Them* (Studio Vista).
Pasterak, Josephine, *Costuming for the Theatre* (Crown).
Walkup, Fairfax Proudfit, *Dressing the Part* (Appleton-Century-Crofts).
White, A. V., *Making Stage Costumes for Amateurs* (Routledge & Kegan Paul).

The following are useful reference books:

Berstein, Aline, *Masterpieces of Women's Costumes of.the 18th and 19th Centuries* (Crown).
Cunnington, C. W., *English Women's Clothing in the Nineteenth Century* (Faber).
Cunnington, C. W., *English Women's Clothing in the Present Century* (Faber).
Laver, James, ed., *Costumes of the Western World* (Harper), 6 volumes
Laver, James, *Drama, the Costume and Decor* (Studio).
Lester, Katherine and Oerk, Bess, *Accessories of Dress* (Manual Arts).
Norris, Herbert, *Costume and Fashion* (Dent), 6 volumes.
Quennell, Marjorie and C. H. B., *A History of Everyday Life in Roman and Anglo-Saxon Times* (Batsford).
Quennell, Marjorie and C. H. B., *A History of Everyday Things in Ancient Greece* (Batsford).
Quennell, Marjorie and C. H. B., *A History of Everyday Things in England* (Batsford), volumes I-IV, 1066-1914.
Waugh, Nora, *Corsets and Crinolines* (Batsford).
Wilcox, R. Turner, *Five Centuries of American Costume* (Scribner).
Wilcox, R. Turner, *Mode in Hats and Headresses* (Scribner).
Willett, C. and Cunnington, Phyllis, *Handbook of English Costume in the Seventeenth Century* (Faber).
Willett, C. and Cunnington, Phyllis, *Handbook of English Costume in the Sixteenth Century* (Faber).
Willett, C. and Cunnington, Phyllis, *Handbook of English Medieval Costume* (Faber).

in Conclusion

There is still much to be said, but this must be left to writers more accomplished in specific fields. I have merely attempted to give a basic, minimum account of what is required to present a play with any degree of proficiency when money is hard to come by. It transpires, though, even in such a basic, minimum account, that there is still much to remember. But then, I hope I have never inferred that theatre is easy.

On the contrary, I know of few harder and less secure professions than those encompassed in its wide spectrum, other than perhaps teaching and writing. These I have tried. I have also spent many hours working with Little Theatre and can confidently pronounce that, although he may not know it, the conscientious amateur has chosen for himself an exceedingly difficult hobby. Whereas the professional can and must give all his time to theatre, the amateur is left to learn his lines between earning a living at something else. Of course, he wants it that way. But he's still to be admired for his creative contribution. If he's a backstage worker he should be admired even more.

Potential performers in the amateur theatre (especially those without talent) are many. Those content to undertake less pretentious work to create an acting environment for others are the precious gems of Little Theatre and should be treasured accordingly.

Finally, if I could offer advice to the young it would have to be this: theatre is an entertainment; not a performer's ego trip.

An audience, therefore, is not concerned with *how* an actor did it, but *what* he actually did.

People are unimpressed by the tremendous depths to which an actor says he emoted to intellectually embrace the many facets of Hamlet. Instead, they want to see Hamlet himself standing before them in that mystic world of make-believe which we call Theatre. It is a world in which passions run high, a world which has the audience sitting on its perimeter and looking on, inspired to love, hate, muster anger and displeasure, but never remaining indifferent.

There can be no better story to document an actor's approach to his work than that concerning Dame Edith Evans. Having just played Ophelia, she was in her dressing room cleaning off her make-up when she was approached by a group of curious people wanting to know how she mastered the role.

"What emotional and intellectual course did you

take to accomplish so much?" asked one.

"How did you manage the intensity?" asked another.

"How did you accomplish so many transitions in such a short space of time?" a third asked.

Dame Edith was still cleaning off her make-up when she said: "I acted it."

General Reading List

Here are some general books on theatre which may prove interesting:

Barrault, Jean-Louis, *Reflections on the Theatre* (Rockcliff).

Barton, Margaret, *Garrick* (Faber & Faber).

Blum, Daniel, *A Pictorial History of the American Theatre, 1860-1960* (Chilton).

Brown, John M. *Dramatis Personae* (Viking).

Clurman, Harold, *The Fervent Years* (Dennis Dobson).

Craig, Edith and St. John, Christopher, *Ellen Terry's Memoirs* (Gollancz).

Craig, Edward G., *Art of the Theatre* (Mercury).

Davies, Robertson, *Renown at Stratford* (Clarke Irwin).

Davies, Robertson, *Thrice Have the Trumpets Sounded* (Clarke Irwin).

Davies, Robertson, *Twice the Brinded Cat Hath Mewed* (Clarke Irwin).

Esslin, Martin, *Brecht, a Choice of Evils* (Eyre & Spottiswoode).

Esslin, Martin, *The Theatre of the Absurd* (Eyre & Spottiswoode).

Gelb, Arthur and Barbara, *Eugene O'Neill* (Harper).

Gibbs, Lewis, *Richard Brinsley Sheridan* (Dent).

Gibson, William, *Seesaw Log* (including *Two for the Seesaw)* (Knopf).

Gill, Maud, *See the Players* (George Ronald).

Guthrie, Tyrone, *A Life in the Theatre* (McGraw-Hill).

Hart, Moss, *Act One* (Random House).

Harvey, Ruth, *Curtain Time* (Houghton, Mifflin).

Henderson, Archibald, *George Bernard Shaw: Man of the Century* (Appleton-Century-Crofts).

Houghton, Norris, *Return Engagement* (Holt, Rinehart and Winston).

Irving, Laurence, *Irving* (Faber & Faber).

Kerr, Walter, *Theatre in Spite of Itself* (Simon & Schuster).

Magarshack, David, *Chekhov, a Life* (Faber & Faber).

Magarshack, David, ed., *Stanislavsky on the Art of the Stage* (McGibbon & Kee).

Mander, Raymond and Mitchenson, Joe, *A Picture of History of the British Theatre* (Hulton).

Oppenheimer, George, ed., *The Passionate Playgoer: A Personal Scrapbook* (Viking).

Pearson, Hesketh, *Oscar Wilde* (Methuen).

Playfair, Giles, *Kean* (Reinhardt & Evans).

Ruggles, Eleanor, *Prince of Players: Edwin Booth* (Norton).

Saint-Denis, Michel, *The Rediscovery of Style* (Heinemann).

Steen, Margaret, *A Pride of Terrys* (Longmans).

Taylor, John R., *Anger and After* (Methuen).

Tynan, Kenneth, *Curtains* (Atheneum).

Whiting, Frank M., *An Introduction to the Theatre* (Harper).

Williams, Emlyn, *George* (Hamish Hamilton).